T0380384

Praise for the novels of Alison Pace

# *A Pug's Tale*

"Pace is the alpha writer of feel-good, girl-in-the-city-with-dog novels . . . a winningly affectionate tribute to art, love, New York City, and pugs." —*Booklist*

"A world-famous museum—a darling heist—and pugs! Pure fun." —Lauren Willig, *New York Times* bestselling author of *The Garden Intrigue*

"A delightful romp through the Met with Hope McNeill and her lovable pug companion, Max. Hope tackles the potential pitfalls of art theft, ex-boyfriends, absent boyfriends, and pug-to-pug relations with a delicate and endearing spirit." —Rebecca M. Hale, *New York Times* bestselling author of *How to Tail a Cat*

"A charming mystery . . . with abundant personality." —*Publishers Weekly*

"I loved this smart, fun mystery with Alison Pace's wistful, wonderful voice . . . and one brainy pug." —Melissa Senate, author of *The Love Goddess' Cooking School*

"A charming mystery that will delight dog lovers and art lovers alike." —*Fresh Fiction*

"A fun lighthearted amateur sleuth for canine caper fans . . . entertaining . . . dog lovers will especially enjoy the return to Pug Hill." —*Midwest Book Review*

*continued . . .*

# City Dog

"Pace exhibits a keen eye for characters, both human and canine."
—*The Newark Star-Ledger*

"A whimsical, fanciful story . . . Pace writes with wit, confidence, a delightful and gentle voice, and a keen eye that misses nothing."
—Lee Harrington, bestselling author of *Rex and the City*

"With a wonderful city and a sassy dog as strong ancillary characters, Pace has another winner on her hands."     —*Pampered Puppy*

"I read the first page and I was hooked. I loved Alison Pace's voice."     —SheKnows.com

# Through Thick and Thin

"[A] sensitive and knowing exploration of the trickiness—and value—of meaningful relationships."     —*Kirkus Reviews*

"Endearing . . . craftily portraying the balancing act between work and play, family (be it four-legged or two) and friends, and food and fasting."     —*Publishers Weekly*

"A tale of two sisters that charmed me, and even better, introduced me to the wry and artful writing of Alison Pace."
—Elizabeth McKenzie, author of *MacGregor Tells the World*

# Pug Hill

"I adored *Pug Hill* . . . a great example of a single-girl-in-the-city narrator who's not sparkly or ditzy, but neurotic and a little sad . . . You hope for good things to happen to her, and cheer when they do."
—Jennifer Weiner, *New York Times* bestselling author of *Then Came You*

"Smart and witty."     —*Library Journal*

"Alison Pace's dry and breezy wit makes this a delightful, funny read for pugs and humans alike."
—Wilson the Pug with Nancy Levine, authors of *The Ugly Pugling*

"*Pug Hill* is all at once touching, witty, and so very smart. I love this nervous and self-deprecating narrator who makes low self-esteem not only funny and endearing but enviable. There's a terrific comedic eye at work here and a tender heart—a most satisfying combination."
—Elinor Lipman, author of *The Family Man*

"Playful, funny . . . the story of a woman confronting her fears and the adorable pooches that can help her do it."          —*Pages*

"Pitch-perfect and deftly written . . . a funny, charming, and touching novel."
—Robin Epstein and Renée Kaplan, coauthors of *Shaking Her Assets*

"Alison Pace isn't afraid to tackle serious subjects, even as she delivers a wry and witty portrait of a woman growing up and growing into herself at long last."
—Joshilyn Jackson, *New York Times* bestselling author of *A Grown-Up Kind of Pretty*

## *If Andy Warhol Had a Girlfriend*

"*If Andy Warhol Had a Girlfriend* is pure, guilt-free pleasure. When you're not laughing your head off, you're in the middle of a remarkably honest and heartfelt story about a woman who has to find love inside herself before she can find it outside."
—Joseph Weisberg, author of *An Ordinary Spy*

"Laugh-out-loud funny."          —*Booklist*

*continued . . .*

"Alison Pace takes us on a whirlwind transcontinental journey (first class, of course) with a loveable main character who, amid the crazy world of abstract art, discovers a little inspiration of her own."
—Jennifer O'Connell, author of *Everything I Needed to Know About Being a Girl I Learned from Judy Blume*

"A funny, feel-good fairy tale set improbably in the high-powered international art world. *If Andy Warhol Had a Girlfriend* will give hope to the most relationship-weary heart."
—Pam Houston, author of *Contents May Have Shifted*

"A poignant and very funny look at the dating life of a fictional New York gal."
—*The Washington Post*

"This book is GENIUS! I stayed up all night laughing hyena-style."
—Jill Kargman, author of *The Rock Star in Seat 3A*

"Art lovers, dog lovers—even EX-lovers—will love this fun, funny book."
—Beth Kendrick, author of *The Bake-Off*

"A laugh-out-loud look at art fairs, true love, and overindulged miniature schnauzers. A great read!"
—Kristen Buckley, author of *Tramps Like Us*

"A funny, snappy, beauty of a read—I loved it."
—Sarah Mlynowski, author of *Ten Things We Did (and Probably Shouldn't Have)*

*Books by Alison Pace*

IF ANDY WARHOL HAD A GIRLFRIEND

PUG HILL

THROUGH THICK AND THIN

CITY DOG

A PUG'S TALE

YOU TELL YOUR DOG FIRST

# You Tell
# Your Dog First

ALISON PACE

BERKLEY BOOKS, NEW YORK

**THE BERKLEY PUBLISHING GROUP**
**Published by the Penguin Group**
**Penguin Group (USA) Inc.**
**375 Hudson Street, New York, New York 10014, USA**
Penguin Group (Canada), 90 Eglinton Avenue East, Suite 700, Toronto, Ontario M4P 2Y3, Canada
(a division of Pearson Penguin Canada Inc.) • Penguin Books Ltd., 80 Strand, London WC2R 0RL,
England • Penguin Ireland, 25 St. Stephen's Green, Dublin 2, Ireland (a division of Penguin
Books Ltd.) • Penguin Group (Australia), 707 Collins Street, Melbourne, Victoria 3008, Australia
(a division of Pearson Australia Group Pty. Ltd.) • Penguin Books India Pvt. Ltd., 11 Community
Centre, Panchsheel Park, New Delhi—110 017, India • Penguin Group (NZ), 67 Apollo Drive,
Rosedale, Auckland 0632, New Zealand (a division of Pearson New Zealand Ltd.) • Penguin Books,
Rosebank Office Park, 181 Jan Smuts Avenue, Parktown North 2193, South Africa • Penguin China,
B7 Jaiming Center, 27 East Third Ring Road North, Chaoyang District, Beijing 100020, China

Penguin Books Ltd., Registered Offices: 80 Strand, London WC2R 0RL, England

This book is an original publication of The Berkley Publishing Group.

The publisher does not have any control over and does not assume any responsibility for author or
third-party websites or their content.

All names and identifying characteristics have been changed to protect the privacy of the individuals
involved.

Copyright © 2012 by Alison Pace.
"Can We Interest You in a Piece of Cheese?" originally appeared in different form in *HOWL:
A Collection of the Best Contemporary Dog Wit*, Crown, October 2008.
Cover art: "Rainy Street" by Tatiana Sayig/Shutterstock. "Photo of Carlie" provided by Alison Pace.
Cover design by Rita Frangie.
Interior text design by Laura K. Corless.

All rights reserved.
No part of this book may be reproduced, scanned, or distributed in any printed or
electronic form without permission. Please do not participate in or encourage piracy of
copyrighted materials in violation of the author's rights. Purchase only authorized editions.
BERKLEY® is a registered trademark of Penguin Group (USA) Inc.
The "B" design is a trademark of Penguin Group (USA) Inc.

PUBLISHING HISTORY
Berkley trade paperback edition / November 2012

Library of Congress Cataloging-in-Publication Data

Pace, Alison.
You tell your dog first / Alison Pace. — Berkley trade paperback ed.
p. cm.
ISBN 978-0-425-25587-2
1. Pace, Alison. 2. Dogs. 3. Human-animal relationships. I. Title.
PS3566.A24Z46 2012
813'.54—dc23
[B]
2012025998

*Penguin is committed to publishing works of quality and integrity.
In that spirit, we are proud to offer this book to our readers;
however, the story, the experiences, and the words
are the author's alone.*

ALWAYS LEARNING                              PEARSON

147204767

# You Tell
# Your Dog First

. . . . . . . . . . . . . . . . . . . . . . . . . . . . . . . . . . . . . . . . . . . . . . . .

## ALISON PACE

BERKLEY BOOKS, NEW YORK

**THE BERKLEY PUBLISHING GROUP**
**Published by the Penguin Group**
**Penguin Group (USA) Inc.**
**375 Hudson Street, New York, New York 10014, USA**
Penguin Group (Canada), 90 Eglinton Avenue East, Suite 700, Toronto, Ontario M4P 2Y3, Canada
(a division of Pearson Penguin Canada Inc.) • Penguin Books Ltd., 80 Strand, London WC2R 0RL,
England • Penguin Ireland, 25 St. Stephen's Green, Dublin 2, Ireland (a division of Penguin
Books Ltd.) • Penguin Group (Australia), 707 Collins Street, Melbourne, Victoria 3008, Australia
(a division of Pearson Australia Group Pty. Ltd.) • Penguin Books India Pvt. Ltd., 11 Community
Centre, Panchsheel Park, New Delhi—110 017, India • Penguin Group (NZ), 67 Apollo Drive,
Rosedale, Auckland 0632, New Zealand (a division of Pearson New Zealand Ltd.) • Penguin Books,
Rosebank Office Park, 181 Jan Smuts Avenue, Parktown North 2193, South Africa • Penguin China,
B7 Jaiming Center, 27 East Third Ring Road North, Chaoyang District, Beijing 100020, China

Penguin Books Ltd., Registered Offices: 80 Strand, London WC2R 0RL, England

This book is an original publication of The Berkley Publishing Group.

The publisher does not have any control over and does not assume any responsibility for author or
third-party websites or their content.

All names and identifying characteristics have been changed to protect the privacy of the individuals
involved.

Copyright © 2012 by Alison Pace.
"Can We Interest You in a Piece of Cheese?" originally appeared in different form in *HOWL:
A Collection of the Best Contemporary Dog Wit*, Crown, October 2008.
Cover art: "Rainy Street" by Tatiana Sayig/Shutterstock. "Photo of Carlie" provided by Alison Pace.
Cover design by Rita Frangie.
Interior text design by Laura K. Corless.

All rights reserved.
No part of this book may be reproduced, scanned, or distributed in any printed or
electronic form without permission. Please do not participate in or encourage piracy of
copyrighted materials in violation of the author's rights. Purchase only authorized editions.
BERKLEY® is a registered trademark of Penguin Group (USA) Inc.
The "B" design is a trademark of Penguin Group (USA) Inc.

PUBLISHING HISTORY
Berkley trade paperback edition / November 2012

Library of Congress Cataloging-in-Publication Data

Pace, Alison.
You tell your dog first / Alison Pace. — Berkley trade paperback ed.
p. cm.
ISBN 978-0-425-25587-2
1. Pace, Alison. 2. Dogs. 3. Human-animal relationships. I. Title.
PS3566.A24Z46 2012
813'.54—dc23
[B]
2012025998

*Penguin is committed to publishing works of quality and integrity.
In that spirit, we are proud to offer this book to our readers;
however, the story, the experiences, and the words
are the author's alone.*

*For Anthony. And Carlie.*

Many of the names and identifying characteristics of the individuals immortalized in this collection have been changed. Some of the events have been compressed and a bit altered for the sake of the narrative. Some things are out of order. Some things have been left out altogether. It's the truth, as written by someone who spends a lot of time making things up.

Before you get a dog you can't quite imagine
what living with one might be like;
afterward you can't imagine living any other way.

—Caroline Knapp, *Pack of Two*

# CONTENTS

· · · · · · · · · · · · · · · · · · ·

Contents

# CONTENTS

· · · · · · · · · · · · · · · · ·

Contents

# (To All the Dogs I've Loved Before)

I was born on Long Island on the last day of August in the first year of the 1970s. I was one month ahead of schedule. Upon leaving the hospital, after a short period of incubation, I went home with my parents to the house I would live in for the next eighteen years (and they for the next thirty-two). I was preceded by my three-years-older sister, Joey; a St. Bernard, Morgan; a French poodle, Mischief; and an English bulldog, Adelaide, also known as the Lady of the House.

My family would grow to include Boswell, an English mastiff; Maxwell, an Irish wolfhound/English sheepdog mix; Winston, a Scottish terrier; Brentwood, a Wheaten terrier; Sasha, Spanky, and Maggie, all three Chinese Shar-Peis (it was the eighties); Jake, a Corgi; Bailey, a Jack Russell terrier; and Jessica and Dunner, Boston terriers. There were two guinea pigs, Henry and Alexander; a rabbit we rabbit-sat for whose name I can't remember but something makes me want to say it was based on one of the characters in *Watership Down*. There were many hamsters, beginning with Simon and Garfunkel, and then after the death of Simon at the hands (teeth) of Garfunkel (and a pet store explanation that two male hamsters can't coexist in the same Habitrail, as we had just witnessed), there was Mrs. Robinson. I'd like to point out that I named these hamsters on my own.

There was a terrible period in which my father took to feeding stray cats outside the kitchen door. Every cat in the county came and sprawled in horridly inbred splendor in the driveway. There was a lost duckling, Nosila, which is *Alison* spelled backward. And my mom once spent several weeks nursing a bird named Yancy. For a number of years, we had a Sicilian burro. His name was Juan Pablo.

But throughout it all, the part that was constant, the part that was the best part, was the dog part. I remember, in that close-your-eyes-and-shudder way, the cats and the second-generation hamsters that sometimes ate each other. I look back fondly but with a sense of disconnectedness at the short time I spent with Henry and Alexander. The rabbit whose name I can't quite place doesn't really show up on my radar. But the dogs: I remember every one of them in exact and stunning detail.

I remember how Morgan the St. Bernard loved to swim

and would troll the neighborhood for swimming pools. A ringing phone often meant someone a mile away announcing a St. Bernard doing laps. I remember the neighborhood dogs who would wander in off the golf course next door, and the names we gave them: Chips. Cosgrove. Clyde. I don't remember why they all started with *C*. I remember my next-door neighbor's Great Dane. She was called Alex.

When my family is gathered around a table at a holiday, we tell stories about our dogs. I tell time by dogs. I figure out what happened, when, in my childhood by recalling which dogs were there to witness.

"Oh, that was when we had Boswell and Morgan, but not Max." "That was the year we took Winston to Nantucket; the year after we got Sasha; the summer Spanky came; that was right after Maggie."

For a bit more than a decade after college, I lived a life without dogs. In those years, I doted on my sister's pug, Maude, and on visits home I grew inordinately close to my parents' dogs. I remember frequent (albeit one-sided) negotiations in which I'd lobby to bring Jessica, a rescued Boston terrier, back to my apartment with me.

Just before I became a writer, one whose jacket copy and reviews almost always include the phrase *writes about dogs*, I lived in a building that didn't allow them. I spent the years I lived there contemplating different ways to spend more time around canines. For better, or worse, my nascent career(s) as dog walker and dog trainer didn't pan out. Eventually,

I moved, and before I'd unpacked my boxes, my search for a dog began in earnest. Showing off to a prospective breeder, I proudly rambled off in an e-mail the names and breeds of all the canines I'd had. I wanted to impress her by how accustomed I was to dogs. "My God," she wrote back. "What on earth happened to all of them?"

"Oh, no," I explained. "Those were the dogs of my childhood."

And with that sorted, the first steps were made in my bringing home a year-old West Highland white terrier, Carlie, whose "show career wasn't working out."

Though I credit my mom for teaching me to love dogs, it is my dad who crystallized what dogs mean to me. On my first visit to my parents' house with a dog of my own, my dad turned to me and said, "It's wonderful, isn't it, the way that dogs connect you to the world." And I thought, in this order, *Yes, it is*, and *Yes, that's it exactly*. That is to me what every story about dogs is, at its heart, about.

As I put the finishing touches on this collection of essays, two of my parents' dogs have gone on what I think of, try to think of, as their "big walk." They passed away within a week of each other, something that might have been heartbreakingly poetic were it not for the fact they were not ever what anyone could call fond of each other in life. They both lived long and happy lives, due in large part to the extremely high level of care and devotion my parents always give to their dogs—though it goes without saying that the length and happiness of their years does not make their loss, especially the badly stunning one-two punch nature of it, any less awful.

I wanted to call this book *To All the Dogs I've Loved Before*, but the consensus was that such a title didn't work. I asked, "Why? Because it makes you think too much about Willie Nelson?" And the answer was, "No, because it makes you think too much of dead dogs."

This book is not about that.

I don't want to make people think about dead dogs. But I do think it's important to remember them.

I used to think that my main motivation for getting a dog of my own was to connect myself to my past, to my childhood that was filled, in so many ways, with dogs. And having a dog has indeed done that for me. But the other thing that has happened, and this is something I believe in one hundred percent, something I feel certain happens to all dog people: The dogs in our lives connect us to our present and to our futures. Dogs have made me more open and accepting of people, more understanding of my family, more on the wavelength of joy.

*Alison Pace*
*New York City, May 2012*

# 1
. . . . . . .

# On the Friendliness of
# My Dog-Friendly Building

I've lived in five different apartments in New York City. Yet until I moved to the dog-friendly building in which I currently reside, I would not have called any of them particularly welcoming. Over the course of eleven years spent in other buildings, many of them quite large, I must have had hundreds of neighbors, yet the closest I ever came to knowing any of them was barely. I can count the ones I actually remember on one hand.

In my first New York apartment, I lived half a block away from the East River, and right next door to people who cooked Middle Eastern cuisine nightly. The alternately wafting, pungent, and overwhelming fragrances of what I imagined to be elaborate and exotic dinners filled my apartment completely and relentlessly. Before inviting anyone up to that apartment, I always felt compelled to explain that once they were inside my apartment would smell like onions and garlic and some other spices and flavorings I had been as yet unable to identify. I often worried that whenever I left my apartment, I, too, smelled of onions and garlic and simply couldn't tell, immersed as I was in the aromas.

Though I lived in that apartment for several years, I met these neighbors only once in the elevator. It was a Saturday night in either late April or early May, the time of year when it finally seems real that winter is over, when mingling in the air with all the pollen is the almost clichéd hopefulness of spring, the time of year when comments about the weather are at last veering away from talk of cold or other atmospheric unpleasantness and toward that moment when everyone is saying how nice it is outside. As I exited the elevator and then the building with this couple, we talked about how I was headed downtown for dinner, as were they. They told me they'd decided to drive their car for the evening and offered me a ride. I accepted.

Their car was a two-seater car and the woman, whose name I can no longer remember, and I shared the passenger seat. As we sped down the FDR Drive, we made small talk; for all I remember, it might have been about the weather. What I do remember is thinking how strange it often felt to me to be in a car that wasn't a taxi in New York City, and how that night it felt stranger still as the car was a sports car driven by a set of chic septuagenarians. I remember that I was touched by their offer, that I noticed that neither of them smelled of cooking odors, that I thanked them sincerely and told my dinner date about the ride the moment I arrived, relaying how nice I thought it was. I can't remember seeing the couple again after they dropped me right outside Campagna on Twenty-second Street and drove off into the night.

In another building, in an apartment I lived in for several years with my closest friend, Cindy, there was a guy who lived across the hall from us who always carried a hockey bag. When he moved out, he'd knocked on the door and given me his e-mail address and invited me to a New Year's Eve party, and I said I'd try my best to make it.

I didn't make it.

In the weeks after he'd moved out of the building, the management company renovated his former apartment and I would periodically go in to check on their progress. I liked looking at the newly installed white kitchen cabinets, so much more appealing than the brown faux wood in my own un-upgraded dwelling. I'd stare mesmerized at the pristine whiteness of the freshly reglazed tub. Sometime before my last such excursion a couple had moved into the apartment, unbeknownst to me. They also hadn't locked their door and it was, I would say, embarrassing for everyone when on my way home from work one evening, I walked into their apartment while they were having dinner. I felt at the time that it would be best not to say anything, and so I left their apartment, perhaps no more stealthily than I had entered it, and spent the remaining year that I lived there anxious that I would "run into" them again.

In the last building I lived in before moving to my current apartment, I maintained a casual, if more-than-cautious, acquaintance with a man whom I believed to be crazy who lived at the far end of the hall. He often opened up all his windows and his front door and then proceeded to chain-smoke in his apartment. This created a vacuum effect down the long hallway so that both cold air and smoke would rush dervishlike into my apartment. My casual and more-than-cautious acquaintance with this man was motivated not at all by kindness, a sense of community, or an outpouring of neighborly friendship, but rather completely so that I could request he not do that.

There was, perhaps most memorably, a man whom I met by the mailboxes and with whom I went on two dates. These dates occurred during the year that ponchos were enjoying a serious return to favor and were everywhere in New York. I accidentally left my poncho in his apartment. Even though I requested, very politely I thought, that he might leave my poncho with the doorman, he maintained that if I wanted the poncho I should come over and get it. I, however, was not right then of the mind that I wanted to see this person again and so, even though I was, like so many other women in New York that year, quite into my poncho, even though it was cashmere, and soft, and the prettiest shade of heather gray, I decided the poncho might have to take one for the team. I abandoned any and all reconnaissance efforts and decided to carry on without it. In the way that the people who leave you know not to come back until you no longer want them, once I made that decision, he did finally leave my poncho with the doorman, albeit a bit unceremoniously in a garbage bag.

That was it for me, neighborwise.

With the exception of the man who held on to my poncho, whose name was Jon, I either never knew or can no longer remember any of these people's names. I couldn't tell you where even one of them is today. Though I lived in those buildings, in those apartments, next to countless other people for years, I knew very little about any of them. Regardless of shared walls, ceilings, floors, laundry rooms, lobbies, I never actually knew anyone.

It was not until I decided to leave that last building because of its no-dogs policy, embarked on an arduous search for a dog-friendly rental building, settled here in my dog-friendly building, and then at last got a dog that everything changed.

The first thing I noticed about my dog-friendly building was a Shetland sheepdog. Technically, I know I must have noticed other things first. I'm sure I noticed that the building was prewar, that it had pretty flowerpots situated on either side of the entrance, and that there was original woodwork detail in the elevator. But the mind plays tricks, and the kind of tricks my mind plays is that it convinces me that I didn't see any of the rest of it until I saw the Shetland sheepdog. She was riding in the original woodwork-detailed elevator as I rode up. I inquired about her, and her owner told me that she resided on the tenth floor and that her name was Colleen.

"Shetland sheepdogs look like a miniature Collie. Colleen is the diminutive of Collie. Get it?" he asked me. I told him I did though I suspected it was the other way around. Then I realized that in my eleven years in New York, this was the first conversation I'd ever initiated with a neighbor.

Colleen barked as they got off the elevator, and the man asked, "What kind of dog do you have?"

"A Westie," I said, though I didn't yet.

It was not until I had Carlie, not until we began to take our four daily walks together, that I fully comprehended how many dogs actually lived in my dog-friendly building. In addition to Colleen the Shetland sheepdog, in the first weeks I spent in the building, I met (in descending order, by floor of residence): Duke and Maxine, a golden retriever and yellow Labrador, respectively; Little Girl, a Chihuahua; and Clifford, a long-legged red poodle named for Clifford the Big Red Dog. They all lived on the ninth floor, though only the golden retriever and the Lab lived in the same apartment. On the eighth floor there was another Chihuahua, twice the size of Little Girl and named Pedro. Across the hall on my own floor was a Corgi named Lulu. I was happy to be sharing a floor with a Corgi. My parents' Corgi, Jake, had the sweetest, most expressive eyes, and the most distinctive way of turning his head to look up at people with (what looked like) complete devotion.

The sixth and fifth floors, as far as I could tell, were dogless.

The fourth floor boasted Louis, a ferocious poodle; Nala, a Pomeranian; and Romeo and Cesar, two German short-haired pointers. The third floor was home to a Brittany spaniel; his owner explained to me that he, the Brittany spaniel, was afflicted with rage. On the second floor were a pug named Cooper and a cocker spaniel named Abby, and on the first floor lived a boxer named Hank Williams, a Papillon named Nelson, a chocolate Lab named Reggie, and a mutt called Paco.

I got to know these dogs. I learned that Colleen the Shetland sheepdog would bark at you every time you exited the elevator. Her person, Steve, explained that Colleen is a herding dog by nature. Colleen believes other elevator passengers are a part of her flock. Her barking is her attempt to herd them back. I loved this—even after learning that if Carlie sidled up too close to Colleen in the elevator, Colleen was not above a dental display.

Duke the golden retriever was fourteen years old, and Maxine the Labrador had just been rescued from a shelter. Little Girl the Chihuahua had arthritis of the hip and spent two afternoon sessions each week on the underwater treadmill at the Animal Medical Center in Chelsea. If given the opportunity, Lulu the Corgi would charge through the front door of my apartment and pee on my bedroom carpet. Nala the Pomeranian traveled in a Chanel carrying bag. Cesar and Romeo, the German shorthaired pointers, howled charmingly, went on monthly hunting trips, and were not neutered, something that drove Louis the poodle wild with jealous rage.

Abby the cocker spaniel on the second floor had not been properly socialized as a puppy, and as a result she loved people but hated dogs and so spent a lot of time cowering behind her person. Both Cooper the pug and Paco the mutt had been rescued: Cooper from a chained-to-the-furnace existence in the Bronx, and Paco from the mean streets of Puerto Rico. His name was selected as a reflection of his heritage.

In a subtler, slower way I got to know the people. The Shetland sheepdog's people, Steve and Arlene, had both recently retired from advertising and had a tremendous terrace up on the roof. In the summer, they had long, lingering dinner parties, the kind where you sit around the table talking late into the night. Little Girl's person, Amy, competed in triathlons. We sometimes arrived home from dates at the same time, and had some excellent late-night dog walk recaps. My across-the-hall neighbor, Camilla from London, worked in interior design. She and Lulu the Corgi left on the weekends for their country house in Millbrook. Nala the Pomeranian's person worked in fashion. Louis the poodle's person was always on her cell phone, to the extent that I suspected she faked it. Abby the antisocial cocker spaniel's person was a social worker. The woman with the German shorthaired pointers had a toddler and a terrific figure. I ran into her once by the elliptical machines at my gym and she showed me a book she was reading about life balance and then, even though I'd been neutral leading up to that point, I liked her.

Recently, I was walking Carlie on Park Avenue and she stopped to greet a fellow terrier at the corner. It was that time of year when it seems real that winter is over, when mingling in the air is the hopefulness of spring and everyone is saying how nice it is outside. As the dogs went about their sniffing and spinning, I said hello to the man on the other end of the leash. I learned that his dog's name was DeeDee, and his daughter, a real estate agent, had found her abandoned as a puppy in an apartment in Clinton Hill, Brooklyn.

"So I took her in," he told me. "She's wonderful company."

I heard his story as we walked the block together, and before I turned in a different direction at Lexington Avenue, I said it had been nice to meet him, and I meant it.

As I walked the block back to my building, I thought about all the friendliness I have attributed to my dog-friendly building, and I started to wonder how much it had to do with my building, or even the people who lived there. I thought of a boyfriend I'd had who, whenever I would talk about getting a dog, would say, "Big mistake," and explain that a dog, in his mind, was nothing but a reason to stay home all the time and close yourself off from the world. I'd always thought he was off base about many things. But I don't think he was quite so off base about anything as he had been about that. What he had no way of knowing—what even I myself didn't know at the time—were all the ways, subtle and obvious and quietly amazing, in which having a dog can so profoundly connect a person to the world.

I am a person who says hello to people in lobbies, and elevators, and occasionally on street corners. I am friendly, pleasant, and accessible, and even though in certain cases I might be tempted to say that it's to a fault, for the most part I wouldn't. And more than that, I can say with great certainty that I was not always this way. I am a person who loves dogs, and having one of my own has made me much more of a person who likes people. I am now, after living with a dog, a person who remembers people's names. I am a person who will make an effort to see the neighbors who drove me downtown again, even if it were only to say good-bye; a person who would go to that New Year's Eve party; a person who would say, "I'm sorry I just barged into your apartment, and my name, by the way, is Alison." I am a person who would just go and pick up the poncho.

Up until recently, I had thought the chain of events to be longer than it actually was. I had it in my mind that my metamorphosis was a long and lengthy and involved progression of steps, and for the longest time, I believed it had a lot to do with my new building. But it was so much simpler. What happened is this: I am a dog person. I got a dog.

# 2

## Can We Interest You in a Piece of Cheese?

The years I remember as the Shar-Pei years began when I was eleven with the acquisition of Sasha, a black version of the breed who had eyes only for my mother. Sasha was followed shortly after by Spanky, a fawn-colored great love of my life, and then later by Maggie, an apricot beauty who never quite grasped the concept of her name, or of coming to the person who called it, and whom in later years we began to call Margaret.

I think it's important to point out here that the Shar-Pei years did not include only Shar-Peis. Just as designations such as *the wilderness years* or *the salad days* surely include more than just wilderness or just salad, the Shar-Pei years also encompassed Max, an Irish wolfhound/English sheepdog mix of exceptional intelligence, and Brentwood, a renegade Wheaten terrier. At the height of the Shar-Pei years, visitors caused great excitement in our house—some might say hysteria.

"Someone's here!" someone from inside the house would say (the exclamation point always heavily implied), even though such a statement wasn't exactly necessary. The dogs, clearly brilliant sages, always knew someone was approaching our house long before a car ever turned into the driveway. And they would announce it vigilantly. (Except for Brentwood, the renegade Wheaten terrier, who often saw the mayhem caused by a knock on the door or a press of the doorbell as an opportunity to head straight upstairs into my parents' bedroom and pee on their pillows. And once, in an especially unfortunate episode, he used this time to have his way with my stuffed bear, Esme.)

The first step after the doorbell rang, and an extremely important one (though really each of the steps could be categorized as crucial), was to herd the dogs away from the front door, down the hall to the kitchen, and eventually through it and out into the yard.

"Outside! Outside!" we would yell, and this worked well. *Well* in this case is defined as Sasha (the black Shar-Pei), Spanky (the fawn Shar-Pei), and Max (the Irish wolfhound/English sheepdog mix) heading, in a mass of fur and energy and excitement, down the hall, through the kitchen, and eventually outside. Maggie, the youngest (and we did believe slightly learning disabled) apricot Shar-Pei, would often become confused and disoriented and, in most scenarios, run into the den.

"That's okay," we'd say, the reasoning being that surely whoever had come a-calling on that particular day would be fine with *just the one* dog. Only the one dog was a crazed, foaming-at-the-mouth, somewhat-close-to-marauding Shar-Pei. And while a Shar-Pei puppy is all wrinkles and cuteness and all sorts of cuddly, that same grown Shar-Pei can indeed look aggressive. *Threatening, fierce, frightening,* and *downright horrifying* are among the words I often heard being bandied about in the vicinity of our claw-marked front door.

There were narrow vertical windows on either side of our front door. Whoever was not already in the kitchen would knock on the glass and look out. We'd hold up a finger; *one minute,* we'd suggest to our guests, before heading to the kitchen to get the cheese.

"Has anyone seen Brentwood?" someone might ask along the way.

As Maggie stood on the back of the sofa in the den, barking ferociously, flinging herself against the window, and smearing copious amounts of drool in a variety of places, Brentwood remained stealth, on his covert mission upstairs, and the three dogs outside took advantage of the space provided by the backyard to get a good running start. All the better to build up some speed and make a much more impressive thudding sound when flailing themselves against the kitchen door.

Now, the second step, equally important, was to get the cheese. Often this was my job, and with a great sense of importance I would take a cellophane-wrapped slice of Kraft American cheese from its place on the inside of the refrigerator door. Mission accomplished, I'd usually hand the cheese off to a parent or someone else in a position of authority. At this point in the process—fueled by the barking and the lunging, egged on by the drooling and the knowledge of what Brentwood was up to upstairs and how helpless we were to stop him—inevitably two or more family members would turn on each other. Then, about a full five minutes now after the arrival of our guest, we'd open the front door.

"Hi," we'd say, and maybe, "Welcome," although clearly that had been implied. Maggie would now have left the den and joined us at the front door. She'd begin to lunge with a great deal of zeal in the direction of the guest. On good days we could corral her into the kitchen, and on days not so good she could conservatively be called a preview of things to come.

"Here," we'd say to our guests as we led them into the kitchen, the *thump, thump, thud* of Shar-Pei, Shar-Pei, and Irish wolfhound/English sheepdog mix making impact with the door providing both acoustic accompaniment and rhythmic greeting.

"Just take this piece of cheese," we'd explain encouragingly, soothingly. Perhaps in our voices there was just the slightest bit of underlying tension, a tension we hoped clearly relayed the sentiment *What you should really do is absolutely take this cheese. Really, take it, please.*

"And take a seat in this chair here," we'd helpfully suggest as one of the white wood and not-all-that-sturdy chairs was pulled from the kitchen table and placed, vulnerable and exposed, in the center of the kitchen. And finally, we'd unwrap the cheese and hand it over.

When I think about it now, I'm not really sure why it seemed preferable to our guests to sit in that chair with a slice of American cheese in hand and face what was on the other side of the kitchen door as opposed to simply saying, "I think you people, every last one of you, along with your dogs, are insane." Yet we all make our choices and somehow, most of our guests chose to stay. They would sit down in the chair—two chairs if there were two people, and then they'd each get their own pieces of cheese. We'd open the door; the dogs would come in and bark and lunge and bark a lot more. Max, in what he surely must have seen as a gesture of great affection and welcome, was very partial to pressing his nose into our guest's lap, causing both the chair and the guest to slide across the kitchen floor. And eventually the barking would stop and the intensity of the lunges would diminish, until they could almost be described, were you so inclined, as affectionate nudges. One of the dogs—often it would be Spanky (as food-driven as he was loving)—had noticed the cheese. And though at times we might have forgotten to mention it in all of the excitement, the very, *very* important

15

part here was our helpful suggestion that the cheese be broken into separate pieces, one for each of the dogs.

The dogs would take the cheese and disperse, and it all suddenly seemed so simple. Someone might say, "Well, that was that." Someone else might wonder, "Has anyone seen Brentwood?" In retrospect, it all seemed a relatively small price to pay for the endless joy and happiness that came from living with a minimum of four dogs at any given time.

At some point, and I've never been completely clear on why, the location of the greeting ritual moved from the kitchen to the den. Anything that was gained in terms of proximity to the front door and immovable qualities of the couch was perhaps lost in the fact that said couch now provided the dogs with the opportunity to jump up on it and be at eye level with the guest during the bark-and-lunge phase. Though on the plus side, if you actually lived in the house and situated yourself on the stairway once the cheese was handed out and the kitchen door was opened, you were able to watch as the dogs rounded the corner and occasionally, just for an instant, lost their footing. No one ever got hurt or even fell, but there was this fantastic exhilarating moment as eighty toenails scrambled for purchase on the hardwood floors. It had a wonderful cartoonlike quality to it, magical, really, if you looked at it the right way.

As the Shar-Pei years stretched out across the landscape of my childhood, I became a teenager. Eventually, I lost the sense of camaraderie I felt with the Shar-Peis at the prospect of visitors. I literally became the person on the other side of the front door: a junior in high school and then a senior who knew she'd never be able to linger undetected in a car in the driveway, who knew there'd never be a way to sneak in or out of the house after curfew. Because there was a workforce inside—at the ready, ever vigilant, *cheeseless*—ruining, I was sure of it, my time. But as I got older, almost immediately after it was a thing of the past, I forgot the exact details of the hostile and surly ways of my adolescence (as I imagine people do), and now I'm able to remember the Shar-Pei years fondly.

There is a very handsome Shar-Pei named Wally who lives on my block, and whenever I see him walk by, he always reminds me. But then, I don't really have to wait for Wally. Merely a glimpse of any dairy aisle in any supermarket will remind me exactly of that feeling I had, when we unwrapped a slice of American cheese and handed it to someone: that it was us, and our dogs, and that was all that mattered. And that clearly, we made sense.

# 3

## To the Left-Hand Side

No dog held a place in my mom's heart the way her Shar-Pei, Sasha, did.

Until Bailey, her Jack Russell terrier.

Sometimes I think she may be half Papillon, but that's something we don't openly talk about. Bailey started out life as my sister Joey's dog. Joey purchased Bailey from Le Chien, a posh doggy boutique located on the street level of the pink-hued Trump Plaza on Third Avenue in New York City. It's the type of store that (for me) instantly brings to mind women in very high heels toting Pomeranians wearing rhinestone collars in leopard-print bags. Not that there's anything wrong with that. But I do think it's bad to buy a dog from a pet store. Most people will warn you about this. Joey, not the type to heed warnings, did not heed the general one about not buying from a puppy store, or the specific one about not acquiring a Jack Russell terrier at all, a breed that requires loads of attention and exercise due to its robust supplies of energy.

My sister was quickly unable to deal with the round-the-clock barking. So she brought Bailey out to Long Island to meet my parents. But really, she brought Bailey to Long Island to see if my mom, the closest thing any of us have ever known to a dog whisperer, could help. To my sister's tremendous relief, when my mom and Bailey met, it was love at first sight.

Bailey's first trip out of New York City proved to be her last. She never returned to the city; my parents adopted her and my sister went on to live a dogless life for a few years, and then she later went on to adopt every stray that crossed her path. My mom and Bailey proceeded on a long journey of living happily ever after.

I was living in New York City when my mom discovered that Bailey enjoyed eating at the table while sitting in a chair.

"How did you discover that?" I asked. Because clearly that was the only question to ask.

"Well," Mom explained, "we were sitting at the table and Bailey was barking and throwing herself at the chair legs as she sometimes does if there's something particularly interesting at the table."

Though she couldn't see me on the other end of the call, I nodded. I knew this.

"And so I said, 'Now, Bailey, enough of this carrying on, maybe you'd prefer to join us.'"

I nodded again. "And?" I asked.

"And as soon as she was in the chair—your old chair right next to me—she was the perfect lady," my mom explained. "She enjoyed it. She even seemed pleased when I tied a napkin around her neck."

"That's great," I said before we got off the phone. I didn't really mean it.

Bailey enjoyed sitting at the dinner table. And from that point on she had a permanent seat at my parents' table for all important dining occasions—holidays and meals with nonfamily members being introduced for the first time very much included.

Now, I have always found Bailey to be especially charming.

It has never been my position that I don't want to eat at the table with Bailey. But there was a time in my twenties that I worried what other people, people not part of my immediate family, would think. I worried about what would happen if a suitor, a love interest if you will, came home with me to meet my parents and saw a Jack Russell terrier sitting at the table. And worse yet, what if this love interest came home with me on the Fourth of July? The one day of the year that Bailey still wears a napkin tied around her neck at the table, one printed with the design of the American flag? What then?

I felt very strongly that should I bring a boyfriend home, Bailey should *not* eat at the table. At least *not for the first visit.* Anticipating my mother's argument (*How is she supposed to understand she has to leave the table when you arrive?*) I decided on a tactical move: I told my mother I'd never get married if Bailey sat at the dinner table when my future husband came to visit.

That worked . . . for a while.

Until I brought someone home for Christmas.

We had discussed it all beforehand, a few times. Probably more than that. Bailey was going to have her Christmas dinner on the floor with the other dogs. With Jake the Corgi and Jessica and Dunner the Boston terriers, and my sister's pug, Maude. And the recently acquired German shepherd mix my aunt (on my dad's side of the family) had found on the beach in Sag Harbor. Like that, like normal people.

My boyfriend arrived at three, and he brought flowers for my mom.

"Oh, thank you *so* much, and it's *very* nice to meet you," Mom said.

I wasn't certain but I thought I detected a touch of frost in her tone. I worried, deeply, that this had something to do with an association, a bridge she'd built between my boyfriend and Bailey's perceived banishment. I tried to put it out of my mind.

After introductions were made, some wine was opened, and my aunt decided to put her German shepherd in the car to collect his thoughts (with the window cracked; he'd been battling with the Boston terriers), we all headed into the dining room for dinner.

Usually at family dinners, Bailey sits in a chair next to my mother. Bailey has her own silverware and my mom feeds her small bites with a fork. The other dogs, hierarchical beings, had accepted this long ago, and would hang out peacefully under the table and beside chairs waiting for the scraps they knew they'd be offered. It was all very orderly.

But that night, the moment that Bailey (outfitted for the event in her red velvet Christmas ruffle—it has bells on it and the holes in the bells are shaped like dog bones) realized that she was not being hoisted up to her place at the table, she flipped.

*Flipped.*

As everyone took his or her seat, Bailey ran from person to person with a crazed look in her eye. It was the exact same one she had when she sensed a thunderstorm. Just as she did when the barometer dropped, she whipped the other dogs—the two Boston terriers; the Corgi; my sister's pug, Maude (along with two surprise guests, rescues she was fostering: Limpy, who limped, and Louis, pronounced as if he were French)—into a frenzy. Bailey ran a fast track around the table, and the other dogs zoomed behind her. Bailey began a high-pitched screech, the one that during thunderstorms I always imagined was her way of saying, "We're all gonna die!!!" or "Run! Run! Get Squirrel! Get Ballie! We are *out of here!*"

I looked around the table. Everyone looked at me. I looked at my mom. I'm not certain, but I think she looked at me apologetically.

"It's okay," I said, at last. The room let out a collective exhale.

My mom bent down, picked Bailey up, and placed her in the empty chair she'd conveniently left next to her, and everything was back to normal. Or rather, normal as it is defined in my family's world.

I didn't look at my boyfriend throughout the meal. Instead of living in the moment, or dealing with the reality of it, I busied myself with thinking about how much worse it *could* be. I thought: *At least my sister isn't picking up Maude and suggesting that everyone pass her around the table.* Because, really, she did that sometimes.

"Is it time?" I distracted myself imagining Joey saying.

"Oh, I think it is!" I imagined my uncle answering her.

"Pass the pug!" I could almost hear Nana exclaiming.

"Pass her indeed!"

As I imagined my family clapping rhythmically together, swaying from side to side and passing around a pug, as had happened before, I made it through dinner with my boyfriend sitting across from me, and my parents' Jack Russell terrier sitting happily beside him. I imagined everyone, en masse, bursting into a variation of Pass the Dutchie on the Left-Hand Side. That had never happened, but I imagined it anyway. And it got me through dinner without further event.

Later that night, because we did get to later that night and the world had not in fact ended, I told my boyfriend, "I'm glad you came."

"I am, too," he told me.

I wondered if he'd say that if the pug had, in fact, been passed. Thankfully, it was not something I had to contemplate.

"Thanks," I said. We walked outside together to take my aunt's German shepherd a snack and give him a walk around the block.

Lovely and open-minded though he was, that boyfriend and I did not last. The reasons why we broke up had nothing to do with dogs, sitting at dining room tables or otherwise.

For a long time afterward, I remembered the scene from that night. I remembered the worst-case scenarios I'd thought of to get me through it. I remembered other family dinners in which we had, in fact, passed Maude around. Eventually, I combined Bailey and Maude into a fictional schnauzer, made it a chapter in my first novel, and that chapter, my first editor told me, was the reason that my book sold.

I've been asked certain questions a lot: So, where'd you learn to write? How'd you get your start? My answer varies depending on what I think that day, because I think different things on different days and I tell different things to different people. Sometimes it's "Gosh, I really don't know." Sometimes it's "From reading." Sometimes it's "In high school, I had really excellent English teachers (shout out here to Mr. Brogan and Docs Erickson and Sullivan). Sometimes it's "I was really bad at sports growing up. I was always on the bench; it teaches you how to be an observer." Sometimes it's "From the writing retreat I went to in Colorado."

But a lot of the time I think I learned about writing from my family. From my family that loves dogs.

# 4

## Swim, Doggie, Swim!

I was doing a few different things at the time.

I was working on my second novel. I was ruing the day I'd moved into my apartment, in a building that didn't allow dogs. And I was looking for a part-time job.

After several days, weeks, a month, of alternating between scrolling through freelance and part-time job postings, trying to zero in on what I'd be best suited to do when not writing, trying to wrestle my unwieldy manuscript into shape, and (mostly) lamenting my state of doglessness, I wondered if what I was feeling was similar to how some women feel when they realize their biological clock has kicked in and all they can think of, ever, is babies. I suspected yes but was unable to say for sure, as the baby thing had yet to happen to me. I hadn't admitted this to anyone. I worried that doing so would make me seem cold and lizardlike.

It occurred to me that though I am not at all in favor of harming animals, actually downright against it, I could in fact, here, kill two birds with one stone. I could find part-time employment that would provide additional income and enforced time out of the apartment each week (for me a crucial ingredient to maintaining mental health) while *at the same time* taking the edge off my dog yen.

I would work with the doggies!

But in what actual capacity would I do so?

The first thing that came to mind was dog groomer. Perhaps it was because every time I set forth to exercise, I walked past the dog groomer on Lexington Avenue, right across from the entrance to my gym. The signage featured a Scottish terrier, and I have always been partial to a Scottish terrier. This dog groomer doubled as a dog boutique. They displayed the prettiest dog beds in the windows, printed ones with nice designs, like the fabrics sold at Roberta Roller Rabbit, a favorite store of mine farther north on Lexington Avenue. There was a moment in which I felt sure that dog grooming was just the thing for me.

And yet there are a great many reasons why embarking on a career as a dog groomer is not the best idea. Dirty dogs, nine times out of ten, really don't want to be washed. A dirty dog, if given the choice, likes to stay that way. Ultimately what changed my mind was Max, the Irish wolfhound/

English sheepdog mix with whom I spent a large part of my formative years. Years five through fifteen to be exact.

Max joined our family when my mom took our bulldog, Adelaide, and poodle, Mischief, to the vet's for their yearly checkups. Max, a tiny little cockapoo-sized puppy—all black with one little tuft of white fur on his chest—was in a cage in the back of the receptionist's office. Looking back, I wonder if the vet's office planned it this way. It seems entirely possible that they did. The office had a stray puppy, looked at their scheduled appointments for the day, and at once—quite literally and very figuratively—saw my mom coming.

"We've got Mrs. Pace coming in at ten thirty," someone might have said.

"The lady on Bryant Avenue with the boatload full of extremely loved and well-cared-for dogs?" someone else might have asked back, gleefully.

"Yes, that one."

"Whatever you do, if you only do one more thing while you work here, make sure that puppy is front and center when she arrives!"

The puppy who would turn out to be Max was indeed front and center when my mom arrived with her own dogs in tow. He was little, like I said, cockapoo-sized. Mom of course inquired about him.

"A stray," she was informed. She asked what would become of him. A face was made. It was not so unsubtle as a pulling of a finger across the throat, but it was not an oh-don't-worry-everything-will-be-fine face either. It was a showing of the teeth, a sharp intake of air. My mom asked two more questions. They were, in this order:

"How much bigger will he get?" ("Not very much bigger at all!")

And then: "Can I take him home with me today?" (Indeed she could.)

Max grew to be able to rest his front paws on a grown man's shoulders when he jumped up. Which he did, exuberantly, a lot. He was lithe, though, slender; for such a tall dog, he weighed in at only fifty or sixty pounds.

My dad describes him thusly: "He was much thinner than you thought." Also: "Ah, Max. He was the brightest dog of all time."

Max was extra-large, loving, and deeply loyal, and looked more like a Muppet than a dog; he was surefooted and athletic, able to leap tall fences, and the heights and depths of his intelligence knew no bounds. Max was, as my cousin Anthony will say about certain dogs but not about others, one of the great ones.

The thing was this: Every summer, a few weeks before Memorial Day, Max would get his haircut. Max's summer haircut was not what anyone would call an artful thing; it was a head-to-toe shaving. He was coaxed into the back of the Jeep. Max, who had the wherewithal and self-control to remain seated in the back of a pickup truck if told to stay first, went lots of places—the beach, town, the shopping center. But unlike other dogs who exhibit great joy at the prospect of a car ride even if the only place they ever go is to the vet or the groomer, Max, brilliant animal that he was, knew when he was going to the groomer and would do his wily best not to go.

There, his long fluffy, oft-tangled smoky-gray sheepdog locks were shaved off. I'm not entirely clear on why there was never a discussion with the groomer, something like, "How about leaving an inch as opposed to a quarter of an inch." Though I wonder if dog groomers back then weren't really the same negotiation-wise, discussion-wise, as they are in present-day dog-obsessed New York City. I also suspect the shaving had a lot to do with the fact that after a long winter Max was really matted, and the options to deal with matting are few. In any case, when Max returned from the groomer, so short, so shorn that you could see the pink of his skin through the thin stubbly layer of fur that remained, he looked horrible. Really awful. We would say nothing about this, not to Max. In fact we would lie, directly to his shortly cut face.

"Oh, Max!" we'd say. "You look terrific!"

"So handsome!" would bounce of the walls of our kitchen.

But Max knew he looked awful. Max, upon the occasion of his yearly summer haircut, felt great shame. This isn't a projection-y sort of observation—I mean, yes, we as a family felt a deep collective shame at the knowledge that we had so fallen down on the job of brushing Maxi that he had to be shaved ("It wasn't just that, it was also so that he'd be cool throughout the hot summer months!" my parents later protested)—because Max *obviously felt shame*. He banished himself to the laundry room for days. He would skulk out with his head held low (his eyes looking up from underneath the brow that the groomer had deigned to leave) into the kitchen at the dinner hour. And for very brief sojourns to the backyard, trips that were only about biological relief, not playing. He got over it, in about a week, but it was always a tough week for him.

It took only a moment thinking of Max for me to connect dog grooming and great unhappiness. It could be argued that grooming was the greatest unhappiness Max had ever known. Or maybe all dogs really hate the groomer and it was just Max who was smart enough to make his distress known, in such a clear way. I knew I couldn't be a part of it, for the memory of Max, for the future dog I knew I'd one day have.

So I began to cast around for alternate vocations: dog walker!

I researched and found a few reputable dog-walking outfits online. I sent out inquiries. As the e-mails I sent offering my services went unanswered, I decided that I would just start a dog-walking business of my own. Entrepreneurial instincts kicked in. I began thinking of advertising and marketing opportunities. Obviously I wouldn't get far in my own building, as my building didn't allow dogs, but I could go to my friends' buildings, big buildings, and place flyers under the door. I could be one of those postcard-ready scenes you see in New York . . . the one person walking five, ten dogs down the street at once. At fifteen, twenty bucks a pop, I could do, as they say, pretty well.

I mentioned my new business plan to my friends and family.

A friend pointed out that I'd be responsible for walking dogs and . . . picking up after them . . . in pouring rain, freezing cold, for hours at a time. I'm not a very good cold person, and this impacted my enthusiasm. The early mornings, the late nights, the necessary emergency availability, the sadness at dropping off the dogs who would surely look at me woefully and mournfully. My mom called to ask me how I would feel if I accidentally let go of someone's dog and they ran into the street and got hit by a car, because that sort of thing could happen.

I returned to my dog-involved employment search on the Internet.

I came across a service with a really hip and artfully designed website that offered people who could take high-energy dogs on runs with them. I had been meaning for years (really, years) to become a runner. The appeal was great, but yet I thought I should probably become a runner on my own before being responsible for the running of the Upper East Side's most energetic golden retrievers, Labs,

Dalmatians, German shepherds, and pit bulls (all dogs pictured on the website).

Next was a place in Chelsea that not only offered day care to dogs but also had a swimming pool for them! I clicked, intrigued. The space looked beautiful—a large granite room with a pool in the middle, large sliding glass doors leading to a lovely and serene garden out back. The place was run by two accomplished dog trainers. And not only did they offer day care with a pool, they also provided swim therapy for dogs who had been injured or were old or arthritic. I watched videos of dogs being gently coaxed into the pool, being lovingly rehabilitated by trainers. I read the bios of the trainers; there were a bunch of them on staff, people who had left careers in sales, advertising, any number of jobs conducted in offices at desks, and had traded it all in to work with the animals they loved. I gazed at the little earnest faces of swimming doggies gleaming out at me from my computer screen, and I thought that a part-time job wasn't what I wanted.

What I *really* wanted was to provide therapy to dogs and also help them swim.

*Baby steps*, I thought. I didn't call up my editor and cancel my contract, but I did send an e-mail to the Chelsea place, inquiring as to any open positions, specifically that of rehab trainer. I received an e-mail back that there were no trainer positions open but that they were looking for a part-time pool monitor a few days a week.

I e-mailed asking if there was a class, a training program for trainers, and what I could do to work toward becoming one.

I received a reply that there weren't any trainer positions open, but there was indeed a position open for a part-time pool monitor. I ignored the *Again* tone of the e-mail and wrote back that I was indeed interested. I included my résumé even though it didn't have any like experience on it.

I told myself I didn't need to, pun intended, jump right into the deep end of the pool. I'd start out as a monitor, prove myself, and slowly work my way up to trainer.

Via e-mail, we set up an interview for the following week.

As I thought about my possible future job, I was visited a bit by the ghosts of employment past. After graduating from college and before describing myself as a writer, I had been, in this order: a receptionist at a contemporary art gallery in Soho, a salesperson at Ralph Lauren, an ad sales assistant at the *New Yorker*, an administrator at Sotheby's, and a researcher at another art gallery. And for six weeks, I was an event planner. With each job, eventually I decided it was not for me. I had a creative spirit and mindset, and I, much more so than many of my more serious, more grounded friends, let myself off the hook about my somewhat frequent changing of the jobs. As long as I was gainfully employed (which I always was), I thought it was fine to test out a bunch of things.

As I traveled on a sunny fall Friday afternoon by way of

two subways and a ten-minute walk to Chelsea for my interview, I wondered about the possibility that maybe writing was not going to be the thing for me either. Even though I'd worked toward it for such a long time, maybe it was time to move on, find something to which I was even better suited. As I approached the building that housed the doggie swim facility, I thought how maybe finding the right career was like finding the right person to love; you had to keep looking for a while until you discovered the right one.

As I buzzed the buzzer, I thought about how once you find out what you're good at, you should stick with it.

A heavily tattooed and pierced and very large man opened the door for me.

"Hi!" I said.

"You here for the job?" he asked.

"I am." I nodded, eagerly.

"Come in," he grunted. I followed him into a stark white entry—stark white in that everything was cement and painted white, not in that it was clean. There was a glass partition, and behind it a dark expanse. I cupped my hand up to the window: At the far end of the space, I saw dogs running around the pool. I listened to the enthusiastic barking reverberating off the walls.

It's like love; when you find it, you should hold on. You should embrace it and cherish it and broadcast it proudly. *I help/watch dogs swim in a pool!* I tried out in my head. *I'm a dog trainer*, I tried; that sounded better. I reminded myself that I was, after all, working my way up. I scanned the room happily, watching the prancing, wet, and shaking-water-vigorously-off-themselves dogs careening all around.

I turned back, expectant, to the man who'd let me in. He was now behind the desk, just hanging up the phone.

"Carol," he said to me. "She's the owner. She lives upstairs and she's coming down now."

"Thanks," I said, and then, remembering myself, "oh, and my name is Alison." I stepped toward the table and extended my hand. He stood up and shook it.

"Spike," he said, and turned and walked through the door at the far end of the partition, into the room with the dogs.

About ten minutes later, Carol came in the front door. She, a tall, slender, muscular (I could tell because she wore a fitted tank top) woman with a pixie haircut, stood in the doorway blinking, letting her eyes adjust to the darkness of the space as compared to the bright sunshine of the outdoors.

"Hi," I said. "I'm Alison." I followed her eyes as she looked me up and down. I wondered if I was dressed incorrectly. I hadn't gone for formal interview wear but had still wanted to look nice: black pants, a button-down shirt and ballet flats, patent leather ones.

"Alison," she said, "why don't we sit outside for a minute. It's quieter out there to talk." She opened the door and exited. I followed.

I sat next to her on a bench and squinted in the bright sun. She turned to me and said, "I'm Carol, by the way."

"Hi, Carol," I said, and I watched her eyes travel up me again, and down.

"Why do you want to do this?" she asked.

"Oh," I said, "because I love dogs. I love everything about them. I'm looking for a career in which I can spend a lot more time with dogs. I'd like to learn about being a dog trainer, or therapist, and your swim center seems like a great place to start. To get my feet wet," I joked. The joke fell flat.

"I see," she said. "You're a writer, is that right?" she asked.

*Well, for now,* I thought. "Yes," I said.

"You're not doing this because you want to write an exposé or something, are you?"

"No," I said. "Not at all. I really want to do this."

"Well," she said, "you don't really look the part. I will say that."

Through the awkwardness, I smiled back at her.

"You realize this is going to be a lot of, well, manual labor?"

I nodded yes.

"You're going to have to pick up after the dogs?"

I nodded yes.

"Break up fights?"

"Yes, of course."

"Help them in and out of the pool?"

"Yes, of course," I said.

"And this is what you want to do?" she asked again.

"Yes," I said.

"How much time do you have?" Carol asked. One of my

best friends had just had a baby and I was expected at the baby naming that evening at five. I looked at my watch; it was two. I figured I didn't need to go home between interview and baby naming.

"A little less than three hours," I said.

"Okay, well why don't you spend the afternoon. Just go on into the pool area and help Spike and Desiree with anything they might need. I'm going to go upstairs and I'll be back down in an hour."

"Sounds great," I said. We shook hands and Carol went in a different door and I buzzed again, and waited for Spike.

"Hi," I said when he opened the door for me again and looked at me funny; there was more than a touch of *Didn't we just do this?* to his expression. With Carol gone I took it upon myself to fill him in.

"I'm going to help you and . . . Desiree"—I remembered at the last second—"for the afternoon?" I ended my sentence with a question. I was now, by way of awkwardness, a teenage girl.

"'K," Spike said and I followed him through a gate behind the desk and then through the partition. "You gotta be real careful that the gate and the door is shut. So the dogs don't get out."

"Yes, yes, of course," I said. What kind of amateur did he take me for?

As the door shut behind us, the dogs, sensing a newcomer and maybe, I hoped, a friend, all looked over to where I stood with Spike. I counted quickly: about fifteen dogs, ranging from a tremendous and soaking wet Newfoundland to a tiny Chihuahua standing with her back to me in front of the sliding glass doors. The pool room had looked a bit more picturesque online. Some dogs jumped in and out of the pool. Some sat in corners.

Another Lab barked without end at the water. An adorable mixed breed dove into the pool, swam its length, hoisted himself out, and ran to the other end to dive in again. Like the barking Lab, he did this relentlessly. The look on his face was earnest, serious, as if he believed this loop he was on to be his life's work. A collie stood stoically on the steps in the shallow end, allowing the water to come only to her ankles. It was insane how high the levels of cuteness in that room were! My heart filled up with love.

A woman whom I assumed to be Desiree, also sporting quite a few tattoos and piercings, threw a collection of balls for the dogs. I waved hi. Spike introduced us. She kind of glared at me.

A large Spinone Italiano who reminded me at once of Max came over. "Well, hello, there," I said as I bent down to him, and he swatted at my face with his wet paw. It was a much nicer greeting than I'd gotten from anyone else. Then he shook himself, dousing me in water and dog hair.

I greeted the other dogs who came to meet me—a cocker spaniel, a Lab, a border terrier, several mutts, a dachshund. Within fifteen minutes I was drenched. I looked around the room and my eyes landed on a basket in the corner: a laundry basket, on wheels.

I walked over to it as if drawn by a siren song. I looked down; the basket was filled with freshly laundered, folded towels. On top of these was a pug puppy. Really. She wore a hot-pink harness. She was snoozing, soft, chubby, curled up on her side, and I could see her round pink belly poking out from under her feet. You know how people will say things like "It hit me like a ton of bricks" and it sounds like a cliché? It's not really. Then, there, hard, it hit me: This was what I was supposed to be doing. This, me at the doggie swim facility, was meant to be.

I looked down at the sleeping pug puppy, so cute she was almost edible in her hot-pink harness. For years, I worked in the art world. I was an assistant, a researcher, a cataloguer of artworks. I looked at everything, always with the vague sense that whatever I was seeing didn't mean what it should to me, and certainly didn't mean enough. But this, this in front of me, the dogs in front of me, did. This meant something.

I thought that it was one of those moments when everything changes. I was, just for that instant, as sure as a person could be.

Then the pug puppy stirred. She woke. She looked up at me. She tilted her head at me, the way that both pugs and people who think that you are crazy will often do.

Two hours into it, soaked to the skin, tired out, stalked

by Labs who wanted balls thrown for them again and again and again, shunned by Desiree and Spike, it was less meant to be. I was freezing and I had to start making my way uptown for the baby naming.

"Hey, Spike," I said after completing a round of cleanup, "do you think you could call Carol? I have to get going and I'd love to say good-bye before I do."

Spike shrugged and headed out front. He returned to tell me Carol wasn't answering.

"Can you let her know I had to go?"

"Yeah," he said. I said good-bye to each of the dogs, lingering for an extra moment with the pug and the Spinone Italiano, who looked up at me so soulfully that I had a deep, deep moment of being sure he was Max reincarnate, and hightailed it out of the pool room.

I really needed to go home and shower.

I didn't have time to go home and shower.

I spruced up as best I could in the bathroom with paper towels and water from the sink. I hailed a cab uptown, and fifteen minutes later I walked into the baby naming. I saw a person I knew from a long time ago. I grabbed a glass of champagne from a table as I passed and walked over to say hi.

"Alison, what are you doing these days?"

I thought of all the different answers I have had to that question over the years. I thought of how once you find out what you're good at, you should stick with it.

"I write books," I said. And smiled. I smiled proudly. The woman with whom I had just shared this information smiled back at me and nodded enthusiastically. It was, I was sure of it, the nonverbal equivalent of *That's really great.* I noticed her eyes leave my face and linger for a while on the right side of my body, just above my breastbone. I looked down. There, across the top right part of my shirt, streaming over to the top of my shoulder, was a long streak of drool. I looked back up at my conversational companion and smiled at her again. I nodded, too.

"I write books," I repeated. And then added, "About dogs."

# 5

## The Hotel Upper East Side

For a long time in New York I lived in what the real estate people call a junior four with my best friend, Cindy. We got along wonderfully. Our apartment was spacious, clean, and we thought, nice. I had the bigger bedroom, I always had someone to eat dinner with, and my life had a built-in trusted confidante to consult on outfit choices and other important matters. I loved that living situation and I would have lived there for longer if we could have. But after Cindy got engaged and later moved in with her husband, I moved three blocks away to an alcove studio apartment in a tremendous building. The building was large and impersonal, but the apartment itself I liked. The layout reminded me of a hotel suite; there was a relatively vast amount of closet space, and there was a rectangular opening in the wall between the living room and the bedroom area. I could watch the television set in the living room from my bed, and often did.

The bad thing about that apartment was the fact that it did not allow dogs. At the time I moved in, I had been concerned above all else with securing lodgings in New York without having to use a broker. So when I found a studio apartment in a building that had its own rental office, I signed my name on the dotted line. But even as I did so, I knew it was a mistake. I wanted a dog in my life. And after I'd lived in that apartment for about a year and a half, there were other things I wanted, but I didn't want any of them as much as I wanted a dog.

I explored that emotional space. I wrote a novel in which my protagonist really wanted a dog but didn't have one. I began writing book reviews for a dog magazine. Soon, I'd spoken on no less than three panels whose titles included the term "dog lit." I was a dog person without a dog, and the way I saw it I had two choices: smuggle a dog in and out of my building daily, or move.

I weighed the pros and cons of paying off the super. Surely a bribe would cost less than moving expenses? I had long been suspicious of what sounded like clanging dog tags passing my apartment late at night and early in the morning coming from the apartment next to mine (whose occupant I never met, yet whose Van Halen I listened to every Sunday morning).

The flaw in this plan revealed itself soon enough. The super was not especially accessible, or for that matter ever around. Also, upward of forty people worked in the building. What did they all do? I had no idea, though their names appeared in vast multitudes on the (mandatory donations) Christmas card the building sent out every year. Any of these people could see an illicit dog at any time and then, God knows what, more bribery, blackmail, eviction, or worse? It was a slippery slope. Further, though I am not against the occasional rule breaking, I'm the type that gets caught. The truth is that I would probably break more rules if only I could get away with it.

And so, I spent more time reading the real estate section of the *New York Times* than I spent working on my book. I set my sights on the Upper West Side. I had always seen the Upper West Side as the flip-flop to the Upper East Side's stiletto; the Patagonia fleece to the Upper East Side's pashmina; the artists and writers instead of the bankers and socialites. I wanted a charming and character-filled yet remarkably well-maintained brownstone steps away from Central Park, exactly like the one Meg Ryan had in *You've Got Mail*. I saw my casual, flip-flop-favoring self walking up Broadway and saying, "These are my people!" And because not finding a new apartment would mean not getting a dog, I called a broker.

"I want a charming, character-filled brownstone near Central Park," I told the broker. I left out the part about Meg Ryan, as I worried that leaving it in might make me seem like less of a serious person than I hoped to seem. I also spent a lot of our initial conversation emphasizing the need for a building with a dog-friendly policy.

He showed me four apartments on the Upper West Side right near the park. Three I couldn't afford. The one that I could afford had a dead rat in the bathtub. I was unable to see past the limitations posed by the rat in the tub, even though it was for all intents and purposes a lovely apartment. It even had a little nook I could use as a home office.

A few days later the broker showed me a fantastic apartment that was, if not in my exact price range, at least under the general umbrella of it. It was in a well-maintained pre-war brownstone on a quiet, tree-lined side street in the low eighties, a hop, skip, and a jump away from the Museum of Natural History. It was right across the street from an entrance to Central Park. The apartment had a beautiful windowed kitchen, a newly renovated bathroom, and a bay window in the living room. It was all I'd ever wanted. (Except for the aforementioned home office, to have one of my books be a *New York Times* bestseller, another made into a movie, a Prius, and a free parking spot. And a dog.)

The bedroom was a loft that one got to by way of a ladder. I could live with this. I felt that all the other features of the apartment, to say nothing of the close proximity to the park, trumped the fact that I'd have to climb down a ladder every time I had to pee in the middle of the night. I wondered about how the dog I did not yet have would navigate the ladder. Though I was at this point unsure as to what type of dog I might eventually have, unsure as to whether I would actually have a home in which to live with that dog, I did know that I was the type of dog person who would let my dog sleep on the bed. I pictured a miniature wire-haired dachshund sitting happily in a wicker basket that would be part of the elaborate pulley system I would rig in order to get my dog up to bed every night . . .

"I'll take it," I told the broker.

"I'll notify the owners and get you a lease to sign."

*Perfect.* I can remember thinking that exactly. In fact, I believe I was so busy thinking *Perfect*, that that is the reason why the next part is a little fuzzy, still so hiccuplike in my memory that it's hard for me to remember quite how we got to it. Maybe I mentioned the pulley system.

"That's right, you have a dog," the broker said. The way he said *dog* alerted me to the fact that he was not as pro-dog as I had initially hoped for him to be.

"Yes," I answered. "We talked about this."

We had very thoroughly talked about this. I had been pleasant about the time we wasted going to see things that were out of my price range, because this broker had the dog thing down. The broker looked at me then, not so much as a man betrayed but rather as a man who has asked someone out only to be told she is already married.

"You know, we talked about this," I reminded him again because I felt it was important right then to really point out that we had already, very thoroughly, talked about this. I had been clear, I thought; concise. I had explained that I wanted to look at anything that was dog-friendly and on the Upper West Side and that while I obviously preferred *close to the park* and *in my price range*, the most important part of the equation was *dog-friendly*. I watched as the broker's eyes glazed over, the vision of a commission that had only moments before been dancing like sugarplums in his head almost visibly extinguishing in his mind's eye before me.

"What size dog again?" He looked not at me as he asked it, but rather out the bay window.

"A *miniature* wire-haired dachshund," I said. I tried to place as much emphasis as I could on the word *miniature*.

"How much does that weigh?" he asked.

"Eleven, ten pounds?"

He took out his BlackBerry and looked at it. He looked back up at me and said, "Yeah, right, the largest dog you can have in this apartment is four pounds." Then he stared at me, as if waiting for me to cave.

"Four pounds?" I stared right back.

"Four pounds," he repeated.

For a moment or two, he didn't say anything else. I didn't say anything else either. Relationships of all different types end for all sorts of various and storied reasons. My relationship with this broker officially died when a few moments later he said, "You know, it's really hard to find a dog-friendly rental building in New York."

I got a new broker. I saw something else.

I saw a million something elses.

I saw places I couldn't afford, places that were nowhere near the park, places with windows facing only brick walls that were Reykjavik-in-February-like in their perpetual darkness. I'd walked up and down Columbus Avenue so many times I felt that it was burned onto my brain. I saw a place that I thought maybe I could grow to like, were I to magically wake up as a vastly more flexible person than I truly am. I learned that a small, green symbol of a dog listed on a website is not an indication of dog-friendliness. This sign actually indicates *pet*-friendliness—in many cases, it simply means *cat*. Or as a new broker explained, "A fish or hamster would be appropriate, too." Very briefly, a very nice and interactive hamster began to have its appeal.

My lease was up. My apartment had already been rented to its next occupant. Time was running out. In my state of mild-to-serious freak-out (that was slowly approaching a state of full-blown hysteria), I called yet another broker. And after I explained, again, the things that I wanted, I took this fourth and newest broker on a trip down my desirous lane, passing by a nearness to the park, the possibility of a home office, and found myself saying words I was certain I would never say again: "Maybe we could look at some stuff on the Upper East Side, too."

The newest broker called me back two minutes later with a small, one-bedroom apartment fully within the confines of my budget on a quiet street in a dog-friendly building, in my current neighborhood.

"Dog-friendly?" I double-checked.

"Absolutely," I was told.

"Are there any restrictions on weight?"

I heard a rustling of papers. "No limit on weight in this building. It is totally dog-friendly. It's a noted feature of this building. With the market being so tight, fewer and fewer rental buildings in New York are offering dog-friendly leases."

This, I explained, I had most recently learned.

"So when can you see the apartment?"

As I wrote down the address of the prewar, dog-friendly apartment that was exactly three blocks away from the apartment in which I currently lived, I realized that the Upper East Side may very well turn out to be my Hotel California. I can get out any time I like, but I can never leave.

· · · · · · ·

My dog-friendly apartment is quiet, light-filled, rich with architectural details—I have moldings, pretty wood floors, and a nonworking fireplace. The building is not without its assorted flaws, but I'm more than willing to look the other way. The goodwill I have for this apartment is easy to trace: A week after I moved in, I got my dog.

# 6

## Carlie Come Home

As I searched for a dog-friendly apartment in which I would live with my dog, I was on the fence as to what kind of dog I would one day have. I'd narrowed it down. I crossed pug off my list because I wanted a dog who could come to the beach with me, and pugs don't enjoy long sits outside in hot weather. I reluctantly crossed off Scottish deerhound due to impracticality of transport and its tragically short life span. I remained keen on a wire-haired dachshund, and on a Westie. Both proved difficult to find, and I had numerous and detailed phone conversations and e-mail correspondences with breeders and rescue groups for both.

My mom called me one day to let me know that she'd read on the Internet that if a person has a dachshund before she has a baby, when she does eventually have a baby, the dachshund will become very jealous. She said she'd even read an account of a dachshund flying into a rage and pulling a baby from a crib. Initially, this resulted in an argument. After a while, it became a private joke, said in the manner of Elaine on *Seinfeld* speaking about a dingo: "The dachshund will eat your baby." I will admit, it (and the fact that I couldn't find a breeder expecting a litter) turned me off that particular quest.

For the record, I never did verify my mother's claims. It was years until it occurred to me that maybe my mom's dachshund defamation might have been based on the fact that a West Highland white terrier, a much closer relation and a more genial dog, might serve as a better companion for Bailey when she or he traveled out to the country for a visit.

For whatever reasons, I streamlined my search: focused it completely on a West Highland white terrier. I signed up with numerous Westie rescue groups. I located a list of every registered Westie breeder in New York. I talked to a lot of people. No one was expecting a litter. I extended my search to New Jersey. After one or two referrals, I found Dierdre, a breeder in Cape May, New Jersey, who didn't have a puppy, or even a litter on tap, but a quote-unquote older girl (she was at the time thirteen months old) called Carleigh who needed a home.

"Is there a reason she needs a home?" I inquired.

It was then explained to me that Carleigh was not a champion. Carleigh was not a winner.

"Okay," I said. That didn't sound at all like a problem to me.

"And just so you know, it's not because she's not beautiful. She's very, very beautiful."

"I'm sure," I said. I wasn't, but this was the closest I'd gotten to a Westie after many weeks of trying. I wanted to stay on this woman's good side.

"She just has something a little funny with her gait," she told me next.

I think that the woman from whom I got my dog is a great breeder. I recommend her wholeheartedly to anyone who expresses an interest in a Westie and sometimes even to people who do not. She was extremely patient in answering the approximately four hundred fifty-eight questions I had for her. (But Carlie does not have something a little funny with her gait. Carlie is extremely bowlegged.)

"That's perfectly fine with me," I said. It was. It is.

When people see my dog coming down the street, walking as if she's riding a pony, they smile. Granted, they could be just be smiling at my dog, but I think they (especially the ones who break out into a laugh) are observing her bowleggedness. When she walks slowly, it's a saunter; it often calls to mind for me the phrase *There's a new sheriff in town*. When she walks quickly, extra quickly, that gait that happens right before she breaks into a run, it's nearly impossible to watch her without hearing a *da-da-dum da-da-dum da-da-dum* in my head.

We went on to make arrangements. I'd come meet Carleigh in person and then, if/when that all went well, the breeder would keep her for another few weeks and I could pick her up as soon as I moved into my dog-friendly apartment.

Because Cape May, as it turns out, is a six-to-seven-hour drive from New York City, we made arrangements for a meet-and-greet in a more northern New Jersey town. Dierdre would be taking her dogs to a show in Ridgewood, right over the George Washington Bridge, the following weekend. She could bring Carleigh, the also-ran, along, and I could meet her there.

I called my parents to share with them this most recent and fortuitous turn of dog events.

"When are you going to meet her?" my mother asked.

"Next Sunday."

"I'd like to come," my mom said. "I think I should come."

"I'd like to come, too," my dad said from another extension. "We'll make a day of it."

I hesitated. There was a part of me that had always envisioned the long-awaited moment in which I'd meet my first dog as something I would do alone. There was, right then, a bigger part of me that wanted my parents' opinion on the year-old dog with whom I would in all hopefulness spend the next decade and a half.

"That sounds good," I said. "I'd like your opinion. I'll come out Saturday night and we can drive to Jersey Sunday morning."

After a brief discussion about how no, I did not think Bailey would enjoy a car ride to New Jersey, a week later the three of us set off to Ridgewood. We arrived at the show grounds, a large indoor arena, just off the turnpike, and made our way inside.

It was just like a miniature version of Westminster. There were upward of fifteen rings, each featuring a different dog breed inside the larger ring of the arena. The atmosphere was relaxed, hushed even, all the show dogs calmly and quietly showing. Then, from the far right corner, a screeching. We all turned and looked at once: It was the Westie ring. We looked at each other, didn't say anything. We made our way down the length of the arena and there they all were: fifteen, twenty Westies.

Screaming at each other.

A show Westie, just so you know, actually looks nothing like a regular Westie, even a regular Westie with a very fancy haircut. A show Westie is very, very fluffy. There must be a lot of blow dryer involved, a really high-powered blower. (I imagine this is why when I first brought my dog home she would run from the room whenever I took out my hair dryer. The only other thing she has ever run from in this manner was a particular and thankfully short-term boyfriend of whom she was particularly unfond.)

As we stood at the ring's edge, I checked the rest of the arena again.

It was very calm, very serene; all the dogs were separated into breeds and showing nicely. Everywhere the eye landed: pugs, mastiffs, bulldogs, beagles walking in orderly lines into their respective rings, running down the lengths of them, standing still for their examinations by the judges. Then I looked back at my chosen favorites: the Westies, the little white fluffy dandelion-headed Westies.

They were still screaming at each other, and now they were attacking! They were spinning around like so many Tasmanian devils and stopped only when they were picked up. Then they completely stopped. The held-aloft Westies looked down upon their comrades who had not yet been picked up, who were still out of control. Each of these quiet, held-aloft Westies had a look on his face that to me looked very much like *hmpf*. My mom stood next to me and observed this scene. After a moment or two she turned to me and said, "Maybe a miniature dachshund isn't such a bad idea after all."

"I like them," I told her. "They have a lot of spirit."

"That they do," my dad chimed in.

I asked a woman who looked official in a Purina apron if she knew my breeder, Dierdre, and was directed to her. Dierdre had a pleasant smile. She had short white hair, not unlike the ubiquitous Westies, and she, too, had a Purina apron on over her jeans and navy blue T-shirt. Dierdre explained that one of the Westies was in heat, hence the upheaval. Carleigh was in the parking lot and we could meet her as soon as the judging was over.

I do not believe I consciously perused other dog breeds. It was more to get away from the screeching; as my mom chatted with some of the Westie breeders, my dad and I took a walk around the perimeter of the indoor arena, from ring to ring, watching all the other much more mellow dogs go about their showing. I noticed that my dad lingered for a while at the pug ring. "Pugs are nice city dogs," he mentioned, as if in passing. "And you love them," he added.

"I do," I agreed.

Next a saluki wandered over from an adjacent ring. My dad was standing with his hands clasped behind his back. The saluki walked right up behind him and kissed his hands. Dad, slightly startled, but composed, turned around and greeted her. She looked up at him, doe-eyed, and he patted her on the head.

Soon enough we made our way out to the parking lot. Carleigh was inside a travel kennel in the back of a station wagon. As she saw us coming she let out a bark, a "woo woo woo." She didn't seem very happy there in her cage, but then it must have been very hot back there. As we approached, as Dierdre let her out of her traveling kennel, Carleigh kept Dierdre firmly in her sights. She wouldn't make eye contact with anyone else, no matter how many times or how sweetly we said, "Hi, Carleigh! Hi, Carleigh!" We each took turns holding her. She ignored us. I wondered if maybe Carleigh was deaf.

Dierdre attached a leash to Carleigh's collar. She handed the other end of it to me.

"You can take her for a walk if you'd like," Dierdre suggested. I took the leash in my hand. "Just walk her around the lot, and if she sniffs at the ground you just yank her up." Dierdre mimed a yanking motion.

"Okay," I said warily, and started walking with Carleigh. My dad pulled me aside and said, "Don't yank her up. If she sniffs at the ground, let her sniff the ground." I nodded. I agreed with him. It is a philosophy that has always stayed with me.

"She's a good dog," my mom assessed. "She's just very nervous."

I nodded. I agreed with her, too.

About a half hour later we said good-bye to Carleigh, who kept her eyes fixed on Dierdre, with plans to pick her up in Cape May a few weeks later.

I would never tell her this, but I was a little disappointed when I first met Carlie.

I'd wanted a dog of my own for so long. I'd always imagined that when I finally met my dog it'd be like that scene in *Born Free* and my dog would be the lion and I'd be, well, the wilds—or more accurately it'd be like one of those iconic final moments of *Lassie Come Home.* I thought it would be major, spectacular; I thought I'd be moved to tears and filled with love. I didn't think it'd be just sort of regular and kind of awkward, and not just because I was in my thirties and I'd still brought my mom and dad with me.

Mom and Dad came with me to Cape May, New Jersey, too. At that point it seemed wrong to leave them out of it. I slept over at their house in Long Island and we left at six A.M. in order to arrive in Cape May by noon. We made good time. I felt kind of awful taking Carleigh away from Dierdre but powered through it. We drove straight back to New York City with Carleigh, a trip during which I began to think of her as *Carlie*. We played her a mix CD of soothing music I'd made for the occasion, a mix that I still have that includes Emmylou Harris, "A Love That Will Never Grow Old"; the Dixie Chicks, "Everybody Knows"; Wilco, "Please Be Patient with Me"; Willie Nelson, "Always on My Mind"; "I Will Always Love You," the original Dolly Parton version; and Anne Murray, "Could I Have This Dance?" We were back at my apartment in New York by six that evening. My dad and I walked Carlie to Central Park. We told her it would be a great part of her life. She seemed wary.

We got home and met my mom, who immediately pulled out her Ziploc bag.

A trainer we'd consulted told us that the best way to introduce dogs (read: the best way to introduce Carlie to Bailey) was by "scenting." Scenting involves taking a soft, clean cloth and wiping it on a dog's . . . nether regions and then presenting said cloth to the dog being introduced. Mom had done just that at home with her three dogs. She'd put her scented cloths in three Ziploc bags that morning.

"Do you think we need to do this now?" I asked.

"Well, I think we might as well," my mom offered.

I nodded *fine*, and then tried to keep a straight face as my mother held each cloth in front of Carlie. She sniffed gingerly at Bailey's and Jessica's, pulled away at Dunner's. She was unfazed when my mom pulled a new, folded cloth from a fourth plastic baggie and wiped it on Carlie's lady places. Then from the never-ending depths of her handbag, Mom removed several new chew toys, a plastic bone, a rope toy, and a Mason Pearson hairbrush.

"For my granddaughter," she announced. I smiled.

We sat on the couch with Carlie between us.

Carlie looked from one of us to the other and across the room at my dad. Without ceremony, my mom picked up Carlie's paw and gently brushed it. She said to her, "Your mommy is going to brush you on Monday, Wednesday, Friday." Carlie did not pull her paw away but looked up at my mom with a look we would both (without even discussing it) instantly identify as confused. Over Carlie's body, stretched out on the couch, my mom looked at me and said, "She's confused about this brushing. She's saying, *What are you talking about, brushing, I'm a huntress.*"

"I think that's it," I agreed. "I think that's exactly what she's saying."

We brought Carlie into the kitchen, where we showed her her water bowl, her dinner dish. I filled her dish with the combination of kibble and wet food her breeder had told me to get. Carlie walked gingerly around the kitchen, turned, and looked up at us.

"I think she's confused again," I said.

"I think she's nervous," my mom told me.

I got down on the floor. I sat leaning against the cupboard a few spaces away from her water bowl. Carlie turned from her dinner dish and padded over to me. She stretched her head up and licked my face, three quick licks. Then she walked carefully back over to her dish and began eating. I looked up at my mom; my mom looked down at me. The looks of pride and joy and accomplishment that we exchanged could be no greater had Carlie looked up at each of us and begun reciting a Shakespearean sonnet.

My parents slept over that night, and Carlie and I spent her first night in New York on my couch. The next morning we all got up, all took Carlie out for her first walk, and brought her with us to get coffee. I stood outside with her. When my parents got their car from the garage and prepared to drive back to Long Island, as I prepared to go it alone with my new, already beloved, but still so mysterious to me, Westie, I got a bit misty-eyed. I told my parents, "Thank you for coming with me. I really can't thank you enough."

And really, I can't.

I was watching the Westminster dog show on TV the other day. For many years before I had Carlie, I watched it. I think of the first time I watched it with her; at one point when there was a lot of clapping, Carlie raised her head and looked up at the TV. Then she turned around and looked at me. I didn't get the impression she liked the sound.

I know Carlie so well now. She is a completely different dog than the dog I first met. She is a dog who loves attention. She is without a doubt smart enough to have known that in the year she spent at dog shows, a fuss was being made over other dogs, but not her. I don't think it's crazy to think that all the clapping and cheering for other dogs might have hurt Carlie's feelings. I turned the volume down that year, but in subsequent years, the broadcast has not at all fazed her.

At the end of the most recent Westminster dog show, I rooted first for the fluffy-headed Westie, and then for runner-up I rooted with equal measures of enthusiasm for the pug, the long-lost wire-haired dachshund, the Scottish deerhound, the Newfoundland, the Italian greyhound, the Bernese Mountain Dog, and the Chinese Shar-Pei. That year, a Scottish deerhound (yes!) named Hickory won Best in Show. Right before she did, the broadcast I was watching at home showed the judge, an Italian judge, as he walked into the ring. Cameras were lined up along his route from backstage to the show rings. Numerous flashes went off; photographers yelled, "Over here!"

It was as if this judge were a rock star.

On that night, in the dog world, he really was.

As this scene played out, in voice-over the television announcer explained that the judge had been sequestered for the last week, without any access to newspapers, radio, or television, lest his opinion be swayed by any media attention that might have been lavished more on one dog than the other. I liked the fanfare.

What I loved, *loved*, was that as this Italian judge walked into the ring, judged, and prepared to announce the titled and honored winner, he stopped and paused for a moment. He hesitated in announcing the winner and instead, he turned to address the crowd. In heavily accented English, this is what he said:

"I'd like to say a thank-you to the dogs, who are very special. I am honored to be here. And I am very happy."

The camera panned as he said it, showing off the faces of the dogs, their bright eyes shining with anticipation: beautiful, special, wonderful dogs. I pulled Carlie onto my lap and hugged her. I think about the words he said a lot. I think those exact words could be said, are said, every day, by anyone who is lucky enough to spend her days around dogs.

# 7

·······

# The Dog Has Left the Building

For the first three weeks I had Carlie in New York City, I never once left her alone. I devoted myself, greenly and clumsily, to telling her again and again that everything would be okay, that even though the show life had been (I suspected) bad, life with me would be good. I did that every day. But I was not at all a perfect first-time dog caretaker; I made my share of mistakes.

At first Carlie and I didn't have the best luck when it came to our excursions outside the house, or apartment, as it were. On one of our first ventures—I'd say no more than two days after I'd brought her home from Jersey—there was what we can call an episode, though I am not altogether sure what exactly transpired. What I do know is this: There was a golden retriever, Duke, and an extremely boisterous Labrador, Maxine, living up on the eighth floor. (Maxine still lives up there, but now has a new sibling, Rufus, the world's fastest growing Goldendoodle, a dog that I think looks much more like a person in a dog costume than a dog.) As Carlie and I opened the door to my apartment to take the few steps into the vestibule to the elevator, the elevator stopped on our floor. Kim, Maxine and Duke's person, had unleashed them in the elevator (I don't judge; in years to come I'd do the same). She had mistaken our floor for her own floor. The door opened and two jumping, barking, loud, big, kind of scary dogs came bounding out at us. Carlie, horrified, screeched at them and tried to run back into my apartment. And as Maxine and Duke nearly ran her over doing just that, poor Carlie peed all over the vestibule floor.

"I'm really sorry about that," Kim said. "That was my fault. I should have had them leashed." She tilted her head in the direction of my halfway-open apartment door, indicating a desire to go in and retrieve the hounds of the Baskervilles from my home.

"Yes, please, go get them," I said, in lieu of a more neighborly *That's okay.*

Mostly I was concerned about Carlie, whom I'd scooped up as quickly as I could and now held aloft, petting, trying to get her to stop shaking. But I also worried about what in hell the two dogs were doing in my apartment. Kim went in, yelled at her dogs, and dragged them out.

"Sorry again," she said, her gaze not exactly meeting mine.

"It's okay," I said. What else could I say? As she dragged her brood back onto the elevator—the only time I've ever seen the elevator in our building not take off on a world tour the minute anyone got off it—she asked if we were getting on, too. (Related: In our building, you get on the elevator when it stops on your floor regardless of whether it's going up or down; otherwise you never know how long it will be until you see it again.)

"Yeah, no," I said, both at once. "We'll just wait and grab it on the way down." I used the time to dash into the kitchen and grab paper towels. I cleaned the accident in the hall with one hand and held Carlie aloft under my free arm.

As the elevator door closed without us on it, I gave Carlie a squeeze, and once I was certain the coast was clear, I set her down on the floor again. She turned and ran in the direction of my apartment door and sat determinedly in front of it.

"Oh, dear," I said. I bent down and picked her back up. "We have to go outside, at least quickly," I began to explain to her. "At least so you can go." I then remembered that Carlie had actually "gone," all over the hallway floor.

Carlie and I made it out that day, though I noticed that as we made our way around the block, at about the halfway point, Carlie picked up her pace and began, quite literally, hightailing it back to my apartment. This made me feel bad because I knew she was scared, but I felt relief for her, and for me, in that she at least thought of my new apartment as (if not yet home) safe.

So for the next week, I never left Carlie's side. Any plans with friends took place in my apartment. Carlie was shy with Cindy, indifferent to Jenn, and she stood on Robin's chest and did her best to lick the moisturizer off her face. I was, for the record, very impressed that Robin, not at all a dog person, was okay with this.

We went window shopping on Madison Avenue with Becky. And then, in a burst of enthusiasm, we accepted an invitation for dinner at Christine's apartment. Christine lives right across the park from us, an almost straight line through Central Park from my apartment to hers, a nothing cab ride.

The evening went well. Carlie was adorable and escorted me to the bathroom when I went. What with the successful stroll up Madison Avenue and now this, I was feeling giddy at this new "leaving-the-house good fortune" Carlie and I were enjoying. Then, we left Christine's—late, around eleven P.M.—and headed out to Central Park West to catch a quick cab home. I think I might have been feeling a bit smug—*my dog and I, we've totally got the hang of this*—as Carlie and I strolled a few blocks before I stepped off the curb to hail our transport.

As I did, I was still unaware that it was a particular night in New York City. It was a night that always happens in New York, almost like clockwork, like the Puerto Rican Day Parade in June. Because it doesn't always happen on the same day, it's less tangible, harder to remember, but that doesn't make it any less real. It still happens every year: the Night of No Taxis. I forget that it happens on the Upper West Side, on a Friday or Saturday night somewhere between one and three weeks after Labor Day.

It is always beautiful, magical in its way. There is that first nip of cooler weather; any last traces of the stifling humidity of August have been clicked out of the atmosphere. Fall is in the air and everyone is back from the Hamptons, Fire Island, the Berkshires, or wherever they went. Automatic out-of-office e-mail replies disappear like summer Fridays and flip-flops, and everyone is in New York.

On the Night of No Taxis, you'll be standing on a street corner, somewhere on the Upper West Side—pick a street, any street, Columbus, Amsterdam, Central Park West, doesn't matter—and you will not be able to get a cab. As it happened I stood on Central Park West, with the dog who'd been in my charge for all of two and a half weeks.

Dogs are not allowed on New York City buses unless they are zipped securely into carrying bags. I didn't have Carlie's carrying bag with me. So a crosstown bus, the usual no-big-deal solution to the Night of No Taxis, was not an option for us. Walking a straight line across Central Park was tempting for its time-saving qualities, but it is not at all advisable to walk through Central Park at—I glanced down at my watch—close to midnight. So Carlie and I walked fifteen blocks to Central Park South and crossed over to the east side there. It was loud: Cars were honking, streetlights were blaring, and people, in this touristy corner of midtown Manhattan, were everywhere. Horses and carriages lined the sidewalk. Carlie looked up at me occasionally but mostly straight ahead, an air of determination about her.

At one point as I looked down at her, I was so struck by how very *stoic* she seemed, how very brave and true to the mission she looked. A few moments later Carlie stopped walking, sniffed at something on the edge of the sidewalk, flipped over onto her back, and rolled, enthusiastically and with great relish, in a pile of something. After a stunned delayed reaction I pulled her away. Horse manure was ground both into the sidewalk and into the wiry fur on her back. Worse yet, it was also on the side and top of her head. Grossed out though I was, there was a part of me that was impressed that in the midst of crisis Carlie was able to devote a moment to her very own unique version of stopping and smelling the roses.

At Fifty-ninth Street and Madison Avenue, I spied something beautiful on the horizon: a taxi speeding toward us with its *Available* light on. In one swift motion, I lifted one arm and bent down quickly and picked up Carlie with the other, effectively hailing a taxi and smearing horse crap over most of my right side. We rode the final nineteen blocks home in odoriferous style.

As we walked into my apartment and I made the executive decision that Carlie needed a bath before bed, I wondered for the millionth time: If it were in her control, would she better-deal me for her dog show days? After I toweled her off, gave her a pre-bed slice of American cheese, and told her, "Another day has come to an end," and added on, "Thank God," I told her one more thing.

"If you don't want to," I said as I switched off the light, "we don't ever have to leave the house again."

We left the house again.

That fall, my cousin Anthony, an opera singer, had an entire issue of *Me* magazine devoted to him. People who were important in Anthony's life had been asked to answer questions for the magazine and were to be photographed for a spread. I was happy and touched to have been included and worked hard on answering the questions during the many hours I'd spent hanging out at home with Carlie. About a week after our walk home from the Upper West Side, Anthony called to say that my photo shoot had been scheduled for that Tuesday. The photographer had envisaged me sitting outside a storefront psychic in Chinatown. Just so you know, I love my cousin very much. (He, son of my mother's sister, is a devout dog person as well. Anthony grew up with Newfoundlands and sheepdogs.) When I think of Anthony and dogs, I think of the time he sang at a private concert a pianist had hosted at his downtown loft, and the pianist had had his two long-haired dachshunds (yes, dachshunds) there. The dachshunds sat under the piano bench, their ears rising at high notes, their expressions softening at pauses, their heads tilted with interest at the audience. When the audience clapped at the end of an aria, the dachshunds, sure the applause was for them, would leap up and charge toward us. A woman in the audience was wearing a fuzzy scarf with faux furry balls at the ends that draped down low. In a flash, the dachshunds snatched the scarf from around this woman's neck and charged, each carrying one end, right back to their under-the-piano-bench lair. Anthony postponed the start of his next aria and remarked happily to the audience, "I think they thought it was a friend."

"This Tuesday?" I checked. "With Carlie?"

"Yes," Anthony told me.

I didn't want to go. I was loath to take Carlie out on an excursion again so soon. Carlie was still freaked out over our Central Park West misadventure. I projected this with all my heart. I relayed our recent misfortune to my cousin.

"So, do you think it would be okay if I just mailed you a picture?" I asked, once I had finished. I envisioned e-mailing off the black-and-white head shot a friend who was handy with a camera had taken a few years earlier.

"No, not really," my cousin told me.

"Okay," I said. We confirmed a time and place, and, not taking any chances, I called a car service to take us down to Chinatown.

When we arrived at the location, I saw that this was not some friend snapping head shots with a digital camera. This was a *photo shoot*, a real one with assistants, lights, multiple cameras, and those giant white umbrellas. As I approached, a woman introduced herself to me as the "groomer" (how apropos!) and asked if I needed any assistance with my hair or makeup. I noticed passersby on the street stopping to see what was going on. I felt, instantly: bad for suggesting I send a head shot, and quite glamorous.

I was directed to the stoop, next to which was a chair upon which Carlie would sit. With the help of the assistant, we put Carlie on the chair and looped her leash gently through the slats for safekeeping. My cousin arrived with the photographer. As the photographer assessed the scene and checked the particulars of the setup, Anthony came over to me and squatted down in front of the chair, close to the ground, to meet Carlie. I squatted down, too, and watched as my dear cousin, one of my favorite people in the world, looked at Carlie for a minute, then reached out his hand so that she could sniff it. Sniff it she did, and then he scratched her behind the ears. She liked it. Her head tilted one way and then the other. And after that, she looked up at him, right at him. I could tell, watching them there, that she liked him. I could tell by the way he looked down at her that he really liked her, too. Anthony and Carlie were going to be friends. I pictured Rick and Renault walking off into the moonlight at the end of *Casablanca*.

Anthony turned toward me and said, "She's one of the great ones."

My cousin, just so you know, is very smart, a genius. I

have always believed everything he says to be imbued with a deeper level of truth. I believe what he said about Carlie, the first time he met her, to be the truest thing he's ever spoken.

I'd like to say that what I said next was something equally wise, something about the brilliance and magnificence of my dog, but what happened is this: There was a loud noise. Carlie got startled and dashed off down the sidewalk, her leash coming free from the slat of the chair in an instant. An assistant with lightning reflexes ran after her and stepped on her leash moments before she ran into the (deserted, *but still*) city street. It was in the nick of time, like really the nick. I ran past the assistant yelling, "Thank you! Thank you!" as I went. I ran up to Carlie, scooped her up, looping her leash five times around my wrist. Anthony ran after me. I looked at my cousin and he looked at me, and I said only this: I said, "Promise me, you'll never tell my mother."

. . . . . . .

Our next trip, the following weekend, was the big one. The trip out to Long Island, to see my parents and meet their dogs.

Or, rather, the trip in which Carlie would meet Bailey.

I rose early and we taxied rather than subwayed to Penn Station and the Long Island Rail Road. I am usually a really good public transportation person; I am conscientious of both my bank account and the environment. It occurs to me that I am one hundred percent less good about public transportation when I am in the presence of my dog. At Penn Station, I corralled Carlie into her Sherpa bag. It was a task that proved more challenging than I had imagined it to be. Carlie was not at all keen on the Sherpa bag. She looked up at me through the mesh, wild-eyed. I thought back to the previous incidents, incidents in which I had imagined it would have been better had I brought along the bag. I re-imagined them. We stood on the platform and waited for the train and I leaned down to the Sherpa bag, hung weightily over my shoulder, and whispered to Carlie that soon we'd be on Long Island, with a yard, and woods, and a beach upon which she could run.

Once we were on the train, I unzipped the top third of the bag, just enough space for her to pop her big Westie head out. I patted the top of her head in the *There, there* manner and whispered again to her about the beach, how she would run on it.

"Ma'am." It came from behind me. I turned to see the conductor looming above us, punching another passenger's ticket.

"Yes," I said, balancing my dog-filled bag on my knees with one hand and reaching into my back pocket for my ticket with the other. I held my ticket out to him, believing that if I pretended well enough that he'd been addressing me only because he wanted my ticket, it would be true.

"You've got to put that dog's head back in that bag," he told me, and reached for my ticket. I attempted a negotiation but he held his ground. I aimed a dirty look at his retreating form.

I scrunched down on the seat and held the bag up at eye level, so that I could look at Carlie eye to eye through the mesh. I scratched the front-facing part of her chest, a part of her body I'd recently discovered she really enjoyed having scratched, through the fabric. I thought long and hard about any possible physical or mental ailments I might have that would enable me to apply Carlie for service dog status. Service dogs are issued bright orange vests and paperwork that allows them to travel with you and be with you, anywhere, without a bag. And surely I had ailments.

It's about an hour-and-ten-minute trip from Penn Station to the town in which my parents live.

It felt much longer that day.

At last, the train pulled to a stop, the last stop on a very long line. Carlie and I emerged, and as soon as my feet hit the platform I bent down and unzipped her from her prison. I made sure her leash was secure, gave her some good pats of the *You did great* and *See, told you it would all work out* variety, and stood back up. Carlie looked up at me, suspect. I started walking down the platform, toward the parking lot, and there was Dad, behind the wheel of his SUV, the very SUV he'd used for years to shuttle his elderly Corgi, Jake, down to the beach, once Jake was too old to make the trip on foot.

"C'mon," I told Carlie as we made our way across the

parking lot to my dad. "We're almost there." I opened the passenger door, bent down, and lifted Carlie up onto the passenger seat. I opened the rear passenger door to throw in my overnight bag and Carlie's much-loathed mesh Sherpa bag.

"Well, hello, princess," my dad said to Carlie.

Her ears went flat back on her head and she gazed up at him. As I moved to open the front passenger door, I saw Carlie's tail wagging double time.

"Hello, hello," my dad said to her next, and her tail kept wagging fast. Right as I was about to hoist myself up into the seat beside her, she let loose a pee.

"Yikes!" I grabbed her out of the car and placed her on the pavement. "Outside," I reminded her. "We do that outside."

She looked up with an openmouthed smile that said two things: One, she already knew, and two, she was already done.

Dad, always at the ready, reached to the seat back behind and pulled out a small roll of paper towels and a bottle of Nature's Miracle spray (used by my family for years and truly excellent at the removal of pee stain *and* odor). Together, with Carlie held outside the scene of the crime, on my hip, we did a quick cleanup, then started on our way. As we pulled out of the station, Carlie walked over the middle console of the car so that she was standing on my dad's lap. Dad maneuvered his arms so that he was holding her upright and steering at once. Not the safest thing, no, but I'll tell you this, it was both touching and adorable. Dad took a hand from the wheel for an instant and hit the button to roll down his window. Carlie moved a step closer and rested her head on the door frame. I watched as the breeze blew her hair back. I watched as she breathed in deeply and then breathed out, a contented sigh.

"We're going to call Mom when we get to the post office," Dad told me.

"So she can be ready outside?" I asked. The same dog trainer who had suggested that we scent each dog by wiping their nether regions with a towel so that Carlie could smell them before actually meeting them had also offered the more commonplace and practical advice that the dogs should be introduced on neutral territory.

"Yes, so that Bailey can greet us," he confirmed.

"Here goes," I said. I, too, inhaled and exhaled, in a more nervous way than Carlie.

"It'll be fine," Dad told me.

I could see the post office, a few yards ahead on the right. I grabbed my dad's cell phone from the middle console and dialed my parents' home number. My mom picked up on the first half ring. "We'll be there in five minutes!" I announced.

"We'll be ready!" my mom said. "Is Carlie excited?" I looked across the car at Carlie, chin resting on the window's edge, eyes closed, nose pointed into the breeze.

"I think she is," I answered. "How about Bailey? And Jessica and Dunner?"

"I think she is," my mom told me. "I told her this morning that her niece Carlie was coming to visit, and she really perked up. Dunner, too."

"How about Jessica?" I asked.

"Utterly indifferent."

"Okay, then, we'll see you very soon."

We saw them very soon. A few moments before we turned into the small rectangle of driveway in the back of my parents' house, Carlie perked up herself and stood at attention. She turned her head and looked back at me. She turned her head and looked up at my dad. She turned her head and looked eagerly out the front windshield. She knew. I closed my eyes for an instant and offered up a prayer to the dog gods—who thus far had always, I was sure of it, really smiled on me—that Bailey and Carlie would hit it off. We turned into the driveway and there was my mom, eagerly awaiting our arrival with a leashed Bailey. Dunner and Jessica were inside. It had been planned this way. We would not overwhelm the young and new and easily overwhelmable Carlie. We would introduce her to them one by one.

I leaned over, made sure Carlie's leash was secure, gripped the other end of it tightly in my hand, and as I did, I thought of something. "Do you think it would be better if they're not on their leashes?" I asked.

"It's going to be fine whatever we do," Dad said.

I rolled down my window. "Mom," I called out, "do you think they'll be more at ease if they're off their leashes?" I waited as my mom considered it.

"What if they get startled and run into the road?" she asked.

She had a point.

"Here," I called. "Bring Bailey inside the gate and I'll meet you in there." I picked up Carlie and carried her inside the gate and into the courtyard where my mom stood and Bailey sat beside her. I held my breath. I set Carlie down.

"Nicely," my mother warned Bailey as she stood up. Bailey walked over to Carlie and sniffed her rear. Then she let Carlie sniff hers. They turned and walked together to the lawn, side by side. Both my mom and I wiped away tears. We rinsed and repeated and did the same with Jessica and Dunner. My dad, of course, was right. Everything was okay, and Carlie had new, suburban friends. We brought all three dogs out and watched as the group of four investigated the backyard together.

"Wow," I said, and later observed, "Well, that was a lot of preparation and planning and nervousness for nothing."

"Well," my mom said, "you don't know what it would have been like if we hadn't done the scenting."

I nodded; I agreed.

As we made our way, the seven of us, into the house, my dad took four dog biscuits out of his jacket and gave one to each of the dogs. One of the dogs dropped theirs. Another dog went for it. There was, briefly, a snarling kerfuffle. I think my mom yelled, "Michael!" I think I yelled, "Oh dear God, no!"

and then it was over as soon as it started. The dogs got along brilliantly, famously, from that moment forward. Carlie went inside and peed all over my parents' house. I followed her with paper towel, a spray bottle of Nature's Miracle, and reminders of "We do that outside." Carlie persuaded everyone to chase her around the couch in the living room. Mom and Dad and I opined that Bailey saw Carlie as a comrade. Jessica admired her. Dunner had fallen head over heels in love.

Later in the afternoon, because I had promised her, because it is my dad's favorite place to bring dogs, my dad and I walked Carlie, Bailey, and Dunner down the street to the beach. Jessica didn't care for the beach and also attacked other dogs she might meet down there. She hung back at the house with my mom, who also didn't care as much for a chilly afternoon walk to the beach and wanted to start dinner.

"How's it going?" he asked.

"With Carlie?" I asked.

"Well, yes, with Carlie, of course. But also with you."

"It's good," I said, and we kept walking in silence, nice silence, for a while. "It's a lot though, getting used to having a dog," I confided after we'd covered a bit more ground.

"It is," my dad agreed. He reached out and patted my shoulder. "But in a good way," he told me. "It really connects you to the world, taking care of another being."

He was right.

That day, for the first of many, many times, Carlie ran on

the beach. Bailey ran more slowly after her. Dunner stayed near my dad, slightly confused. Carlie ran across the field at full speed ahead and circled back. She ran in a figure eight. Six years in, I'm a firm believer that Carlie runs in a figure eight when she wants to communicate joy to me. That day was the day the theory began. Another neighborhood dog came down to the beach: Ramses, a black greyhound rescue. Carlie chased him, while Bailey screech-barked from the sidelines.

Then Carlie rolled in a large pile of goose shit.

Later, as Carlie sat on the ottoman to my mom's chair, an L.L.Bean plaid car blanket underneath her, she was panting, slightly out of breath, and you know how people will tell you that dogs smile, and that that is one hundred percent true? Right then, Carlie had the biggest smile I'd seen. My dad walked the few steps over to her and patted her on the top of her head. She gazed up at him, so fondly.

"I know," he told her. "I know. You thought you lost your family. But now you have another."

# 8

## Found Poem

It occurred to me one day that I didn't know all the names of my cousin-dogs from North Carolina. I e-mailed my aunt Susie to say hi and ask her the names of all her dogs. This was her response:

Hi Ali,

**LaVerne**—graduate school—Cocker Spaniel—didn't like her

**Mona**—graduate school—mixed breed, large black dog, from "Orphans of the Storm"—one of my favorites

Alison Pace

**Sam**—and all others to follow at Duke—Samoyed—first
dog with Phil—she got hit by a car . . . awful
**Jenny I**—Newfie—rescued from horrible situation, was
crazy
**Jenny II**—Newfie—got from horrible breeder when I was
nine months pregnant—took her back to breeder
**Emily**—Old English Sheep dog—one of my favorites
**Murray**—Samoyed—didn't like him
**Ruby**—Flat Coated Retriever—terribly stupid, Emily
hated her
**Roxanne**—Newfie
**Clousseau**—Newfie—one of my favorites—died a
premature death from liver problems
**Ella**—Newfie—very bad problem with her legs—lived
long life
**Marcella**—one of my favorites

Love,
S


p.s. When I moved to North Carolina in 1973, I rented a
house in a cute neighborhood, and then drove down from
Chicago with 5 cats (Burgess, Clancy, David [a girl], Pretty
One, Frazier [a Persian, the others were Siamese]), and
Mona and LaVerne. The dogs roamed around the neigh-
borhood with other dogs, and LaVerne got very friendly

86

with a woman around the block. They loved each other, and eventually I let the woman have her. It was a load off for Mona; she was the leader of all the dogs in the neighborhood. She had many friends, and she wasn't keen on having to round up LaVerne all the time.

# 9

### Carlie Is Ready for Her Close-Up

In winter, Carlie wears a Black Watch plaid collar and leash. I ordered it from a website, puppydogplaids.com. There, a great variety of plaids are displayed from which you can select the particular tartan that best reflects your canine's unique individuality. Someone in Central Park told me about it; she, too, had a Westie.

When the weather gets warmer, I switch over to what I refer to as Carlie's "spring look." It's a light purple collar and leash adorned with bright green palmetto trees. This choice is less because Carlie and I have any attachment to South Carolina or palmetto trees, and more because I like the color combination. That said, I don't believe in dressing up dogs. Though I will admit that when I was invited to be a guest judge at the annual New York City pug Halloween costume contest, I did go on etsy.com and buy Carlie a Dracula costume. I found the entire experience vastly more enjoyable than I would have guessed. And I have some great pictures.

That's actually where I'm going with this.

But before I do, let me just relay that Carlie has but one Fair Isle sweater that works well for her when the weather dips into the teens. The last extravagance I can remember buying for her is a high-end dog shampoo and conditioner. It was offered in three scents: park, woods, and ocean. I selected park, as I felt it was most descriptive of her lifestyle and/or interests. So, aside from shampoo, dog food, and low-calorie dog treats (because Carlie has been accused by two different vets of being "chunky") and rubber balls, and Carlie's yearly teeth cleaning (that is, really, as they say, a whole other story), I don't think I spend an inordinate amount of money on my dog.

It was not always this way. When I first got Carlie, I found myself completely unable to stop buying her everything. I amassed a collection of (now neglected) plush toys that includes a busy bee (an actual bee, I might add, not a bear in a bee costume), something that may have been a turtle and is known as Green Beast, and two soft red balls, one emblazoned in sparkly silver writing with the word *naughty* and the other with the word *nice*, both presented to Carlie at her first Christmas. (Upon receipt of this gift on Christmas morning, when my parents' Boston terrier, Dunner, took a casual interest in the *nice* ball, Carlie viciously attacked him.)

There were several coats purchased before I settled in with the Fair Isle sweater, most memorably a Barbour jacket, which I wish she had not outgrown. There was a hot-pink raincoat with lime-green piping that, preppy though my sartorial tastes do run, crossed a line even for me, and became a purchase I looked back on with regret.

In slimmer times, there were a variety of dog treats, dog chews, petrified cow tendon and pigs' ears and bulls' penises, which apparently dogs really enjoy gnawing upon.

There were organic dog treats, freeze-dried liver, and any number of vet bills and a prescription dog food for dogs with sensitive stomachs—a condition that had not been at all well served by the smorgasbord of food I presented to Carlie, or the doggie buffet that much of Lexington Avenue has turned out to be. There were dog beds, one for each room of my two-room apartment, and bouncing balls to throw for her in the park.

In the early days, I wanted all these things, not only for Carlie, but for myself.

I wouldn't have thought I associated things with love, but with Carlie, in those early days, I might have. And it was like that with the portrait I had to have taken of her.

When I first met my first editor, also named Allison but with the traditional extra *l*, and we were editing my first novel lo these many years ago, she'd just finished work on a book of beautiful black-and-white photographs of Italian greyhounds by the dog photographer Amanda Jones. In the years following, there were additional volumes on dachshunds, French bulldogs, and mutts. Whenever a new book came out I bought it, put it on my coffee table, gazed at it fondly, and dreamed of the day I'd have a dog of my own. The distance between daydreaming about my own dog and daydreaming about my own dog's portrait by Amanda Jones: A huge leap it was not.

After I'd had Carlie for about a year, I told Allison about my deep and heartfelt desire to have an Amanda Jones portrait of Carlie, even though an Amanda Jones portrait does not come cheap.

"You could always write about it," Allison suggested. It made so much sense! It's been the answer to so many things in my life: Write about it.

In retrospect I believe that Allison meant *Write about it*, in an explore-it-and-see-where-your-feelings-take-you sort of way. That's not what I did. I'd written at the time for a dog magazine or two; I'd contributed to a website. I was trying hard to write for more magazines and I admired Amanda; I really did want to write about her. I would *write* about my experience visiting her, and then I could justify the cost of the portrait, because it would simultaneously launch my canine journalism career. Win-win!

I wrote to Amanda and asked if I could come up to her studio in the Berkshires and interview her, and also get a portrait taken of Carlie. She said absolutely, and also invited me to observe her next photo session in New York City, during which six dogs (and in some cases their people) would be photographed.

For weeks I went to sleep with visions of Carlie running through a field of wildflowers on a bucolic fall day in Massachusetts, as the click-click of a camera went off in the background. I booked lodging at a dog-friendly bed-and-breakfast in the Berkshires. I went online and rented a Prius.

On the day before we left, I took Carlie six blocks up Lexington Avenue to Canine Styles, the poshest of dog groomers on the Upper East Side, to get a bath. Though I am no stranger to giving Carlie a bath. Should you ever find yourself with a dog who loves nothing so much as smearing herself across the sidewalk, a dog who happens to be white, you, too, will be no stranger to giving your dog a bath. However, for the occasion of Carlie's Amanda Jones photo shoot, an expert shampoo was in order. Also, a nice fluffing.

When I handed her leash over to the groomer, Carlie glared at me. I inquired about a hunter-green horse blanket–style dog jacket—charming, quilted, with little crisscrossing straps and silver buckles—on display right by the cash register.

"You should get it. It would look fantastic on her," the eagle-eyed clerk behind the counter told me.

"I'll definitely think about it," I said. I averted my eyes and hurried from the shop as they led Carlie away.

When I returned a few hours later, I didn't notice that the green horse blanket–style jacket was no longer on display. "Oh, yes, Westie." The woman behind the counter nodded and smiled at me. "She looks great."

A door to the back opened. A man in what I think could best be described as a white version of surgical scrubs emerged carrying Carlie. She was outfitted for her exit in the green horse blanket–style dog jacket. Savvy salesmanship on the part of the woman behind the counter.

And I have to say, it might have worked.

In different circumstances. But I barely noticed the blanket; the cuteness of how they thought to put it on her barely even registered. Those little silver buckles meant nothing to me. Because Carlie looked, well, totally *weird*. Fluffy, yes, maybe too fluffy, but that wasn't my problem: Carlie looked a little fierce around the eyes. The hair around her snout also seemed to have taken a new direction . . . the pieces in the front were longer than the rest of it. It was a look that when photographed and e-mailed to my mother elicited the description, "Very Fu Manchu."

"What happened here?" I asked. I heard the way I sounded as I asked it.

I sounded exactly the way I had in Central Park one day when I saw Carlie emerging from behind a tree looking very pleased with herself, covered in what I'm pretty sure was human feces.

"I trimmed her up around the eyes!" White Scrubs told me.

I stared at him. You know that first instant when you look at a new haircut and realize it is a layered nightmare? I knew the feeling well. I've hated a lot of haircuts, but I've never thrown a fit in a salon. A bad haircut is a sorrow that must be borne alone; flipping out over it or even expressing displeasure doesn't really help. Though this wasn't *my* hair. And it was the eve of a professional portrait with a world famous dog photographer!

"I took off a little around her snout!"

I wondered, *What was so hard to understand about just a bath and a fluffing? You know, that goddamn level of fluffing I'm unable to achieve in my own home because my dog hates the hair dryer?*

"No extra charge," the woman behind the counter said, glancing horse blanket–ward.

I unbuckled the horse blanket and grudgingly paid our significant bill. Dog grooming in New York City is insane. Then we marched from the store.

I have certain things that I say over and over again to Carlie. One of the leading numbers in my conversational arsenal is a question: "Who's my gorgeous, gorgeous girl?" A rhetorical question, but Carlie seems to enjoy it. I always ask this when I pick her up from grooming; I feel it lessens the sting of getting left there, of having to have gone through the ordeal in the first place. I don't mind that I'm the crazy lady on the street, stopping every few steps and caterwauling at my dog.

But shameless though I am with my dog, that day it was hard to keep a straight face. I soldiered bravely ahead, and as Carlie and I stopped at a light on the northeast corner of Seventy-ninth Street and Lexington Avenue, my gaze fell for a moment on the florist's on the opposite corner, on an entire north-facing window filled with white orchids. Then I looked down at Carlie, and I asked her, softer than I usually do, "How's my gorgeous, gorgeous girl?"

Carlie looked up at me, annoyed. And fierce.

I looked at Carlie and her freakish haircut. I thought about the fact that it would be immortalized in film. I tried to distract myself and grant myself the serenity to accept the things I cannot change.

. . . . . . .

Right before going to sleep that night, I gazed down at my still fierce-looking (even in slumber) terrier. I got out of bed and slipped my safety scissors, the kind that don't have sharp ends and could be used for things like cutting the hair around your dog's face, into my toiletry bag. Though even as I did it I was aware of the very possible negative consequences, the dire results that could occur from taking matters into my own hands.

I did not rise the next day to discover that the reset button I have so very many times wanted to press had finally been pressed. My dog still looked freakish. But the sun was shining, and the open road beckoned, so off we went.

There's a thing about the open road. It takes a while to get from New York City to it. And also, there's a thing with the exits on the Major Deegan Expressway. They go down to 1 and then start again. So, when MapQuest tells you Exit 1, what it actually means is the second Exit 1, but it doesn't say that. No. As if it were a magnet, Yankee Stadium pulled me toward it again and again. I kept getting off at its exit, driving around, not seeing the next road on my printed directions, and getting back on. Like the island on *Lost,* it was as if Manhattan wanted me back. Carlie sat in the passenger seat, looking up at me with concern. Or maybe it was just the haircut.

Eventually, weary of driving around the Bronx, I pulled over at a police station and asked directions. I also called Amanda to tell her we'd most likely be late.

"I love it when New Yorkers rent cars and try to get out of the city but can't!" Amanda exclaimed. I laughed, but not on the inside.

A long drive on a somewhat open road later, Carlie and I checked into the dog-friendly bed-and-breakfast and walked across the street to MASS MoCA to meet Amanda and her assistant at her studio. We had Mexican for dinner nearby and sat outside so Carlie could join us. We ordered margaritas, and I confessed my distress at Carlie's haircut.

"It happens more than you'd think," Amanda told me. It was not a solace.

Back in the hotel room, tipsy from margaritas, it occurred to me that the situation could be improved if I gave Carlie a bath. I didn't have any dog or baby shampoo so I thought, *Maybe if I just wetted her down . . .*

The tub in the B&B was encased in glass. I couldn't reach over the edge. In order to wet down Carlie, I had to get into the tub with her. The wetting down didn't have the desired effect. Dripping water across the room, I got the scissors from my bag.

"Mommy's sorry she's so crazy," I said, as I held Carlie's snout in my hands and snipped, looking side to side to check for evenness.

. . . . . . .

I often think of alternate careers I'd like to have. Many appeal. The next morning at Amanda's studio, as I sat off to the side with my notebook and watched as her assistant rolled out a bright white paper backdrop, checked camera equipment, and set up a large-screened laptop, I wanted to move to Massachusetts and be Amanda's helper.

As soon as the set was ready, Carlie walked gingerly to its exact center.

I didn't take notes and I didn't snap photographs. I didn't look at the scene through a writerly lens. I just watched. Carlie was a natural. She knew she was being photographed;

it has been my belief ever since that day that Carlie is very aware of what a camera does and what happiness it brings. She looked backward over her shoulder. She raised her chin skyward. She gamely ran after bounced tennis balls. When Amanda held her camera in front of her to check something, Carlie went over to investigate, possibly assist. When Amanda's assistant's dog, Milo, scooted onto the photo shoot, Carlie moved to the back of the frame, clearly, obviously, anyone could see it, horrified.

Amanda made a noise like a cat, and when that didn't get a response she asked, "Do you want to go for a ride in a car?" and "Where's the squirrel?" At one point she brandished a rubber chicken. Carlie *loved* it. I watched her, so joyous, so in the moment, so happy, and I thought how much I loved her.

Along with "Who's my gorgeous, gorgeous girl?" I also often say to Carlie, "You are an amazing, amazing animal." I think it started that day.

Amanda asked if I wanted to get in the shots. I wasn't sure. She said we could get one to use for my author photo. I put on lipstick. I took off my shoes, and, feeling tremendously awkward and not at all at ease, I sat next to Carlie. In a brazen attempt to channel a picture Amanda had shown me of a beautiful woman sprawled on the floor with her Rhodesian ridgeback, I sprawled across the paper. It did not have the desired effect. I said, "What do you think if we take a couple with Carlie over my shoulder?" I rotated myself around.

That picture from the back, with Carlie looking over my shoulder, has become my favorite. Carlie looks fierce.

We drove the scenic route home on an outstandingly spectacular fall day, unseasonably warm but still crisp and fresh and humidity free. As I zipped up and down picturesque hills, dotted with farmhouses, with my dog nestled in the passenger seat, her chin resting on the armrest between us, as we stopped for a late lunch and had a picnic in a field—a field just like I'd imagined—and Carlie bounded through it, it was one of those afternoons that I look back on as one of the great moments, as one of my favorite days.

I didn't place my story with a magazine. But I did get my Amanda Jones portrait of Carlie. I selected a three-quarter view, and unless you know to look for it, she doesn't look very Fu Manchu at all. The picture is as beautiful in its execution as the subject is in her spirit. It hangs in a place where, if I'm sitting on my couch and I look up, I see it. It, and the memory of the day it was taken, always makes me smile.

There was an evening around last Christmas when I was sitting on the floor of my apartment, right in front of my fireplace, busy wrapping presents. Carlie, true to the first description I'd ever heard of her—ambitious, busy—is always an earnest participant in any sort of gift wrapping. From the moment I take down my gift-wrapping basket, Carlie is engaged. She's the same when a package arrives. She's up off her favorite spot on the couch or unfurled from her dog bed with her big Westie head hovering over the basket, shifting from side to side like those commercials in which you're supposed to be watching people watching tennis matches as I remove tape, scissors, ribbon, and folded paper.

That night as I concentrated on the measuring, folding, and cutting of my task, I wasn't paying any attention to Carlie. But as I wrapped, Carlie walked around the pile of presents and wedged herself into the (nonworking) fireplace. She sidled up behind a large wrapped box resting lengthwise on the floor and rested her chin on it and gazed up at me: *I'm so much more interesting than these boxes.* My iPhone was by my side. I reached for it and snapped a photo. Carlie, already proven to be a supermodel, a camera hound if ever there was one, didn't even blink or move an inch as I snapped a few more. I forgot about the wrapping.

I kissed my dog and told her, as I am often wont to do, that she was a magnificent, magnificent animal. I e-mailed the photo to my mom and dad, the people who loved Carlie almost as much as I did. I e-mailed it to a friend having a hard time who I thought could use a pick-me-up. I sent it to a few people who might not have needed a pick-me-up, but who wouldn't want one? Buoyed, spurred by the e-mails that came back: *Beautiful Carlie! Bella Carlie! Oh, Ali, thanks, that totally made my night. You should use that for your Christmas card next year!* I posted the photo to Facebook and Twitter and reveled in the slew of delighted comments that came in. Because of Carlie: an hour of pure joy. One hour, that is, in the hours and hours of joy she has given.

In my vast collection, I have pictures of Carlie in Central Park in her Fair Isle sweater, flipped over on her back with her legs splayed in four different directions like a cartoon character, one that could be accompanied by a "Yippee!" speech bubble. I have Carlie wedged between the back of the couch and the cushion so that she appears to be sitting upright, gazing out the window, the late-afternoon sun streaming in through the windows and bathing her in light; a picture of her on a hiking trip outfitted in her hiking harness standing at the base of what looks like a giant redwood, all her focus and attention directed upward at what must surely have been a squirrel; one where she's sitting on a club chair looking either annoyed or as if she has a case of stomach upset; wearing a red bandanna with her friend Audrey in Riverside Park; drinking water from a fountain as a perplexed bulldog looks on; and countless, countless others. I love these pictures, each of them. They reach me, in a different but not entirely dissimilar way from the time when a fellow writer posted a picture on Facebook of her dog who had just passed away—a rear view of a Scottish terrier sitting on a beach, staring out to sea—and I burst into tears. And how, when a friend of mine told me he had an entire folder on his iPad devoted to pictures of his dogs, I fell just a little bit in love with him.

Someone asked me once how much a portrait like the one I have of Carlie costs. I told her the approximate retail price (not including the car rental, the bed-and-breakfast, and the haircut-induced dark night of the soul).

"Is that worth it?" she asked me.

"Yes," I said, right away. "It's worth it."

And here's the thing about pictures of dogs, pictures you take, and post and save and share. Pictures you frame and put on your mantel, pictures you save in special folders on your iPad, e-mail to friends, use as the lock screen on your cell phone, plot for ten months for, drive across New York and Massachusetts in a Prius for, and mat in beautiful archival paper and an art gallery–worthy frame. It's worth it. It's the same thing with the leashes and harnesses and plush toys and rubber balls and plastic contraptions you can buy so that you can throw those rubber balls farther, and rain coats, and winter jackets, and those little balloon booties that protect city dogs from the salt put down on sidewalks to melt snow and ice, to the vet bills and the dental-cleaning bills, bills that are gigantic and unfortunately yearly if your dog has (as mine does) a touch of gingivitis, the occasional Halloween costume, the dried pig's ear, the petrified bull schlong. It's all worth it.

I sit on my couch and look across the room at my Amanda Jones portrait. Carlie's there on the floor beside me, sometimes up on the sofa next to me, and sometimes even in the other room in her bed, taking a moment or two for herself. And she's there on the wall in front of me, too, in a three-quarter view looking a bit wistfully off into the middle distance, and I think of driving through Columbia County on the most beautiful crisp fall day I can imagine, zooming up and down hills, hugging the turns of curving picture-perfect country roads with the windows of my Prius wide open, the country music playing, and my dog beside me, her head out the window, the wind blowing her hair back. Someone told me once that a camera allows you to slow down, to pay attention, to see how beautiful things in the world are, to see how beautiful the world can be. Here's the truth: The same, verbatim, can be said about a dog.

# 10

## You Remind Me of Someone

I knew about Ian before there was an Ian. One winter morning, I was walking with Carlie in Central Park, when up at the top of the Great Lawn a woman came over and told me that she was getting a Westie in the spring. She planned to call him Ian. She explained that she'd always had Westies and had lost her last one that fall, and was waiting until the spring to get a puppy.

I enthusiastically recommended Carlie's breeder, a lovely woman from Cape May, New Jersey, who bred and raised her Westies, all of them, happy, bright eyed, and beautiful, in her home.

This woman, however, mentioned a breeder she'd been in contact with in Maryland. Though it is a great challenge for me to process how someone desirous of a Westie could be in the presence of Carlie and not want an exact replica, I did not feel it was my place to press the issue. Instead, I asked if her previous Westies had not been "good leash walkers." Or if her Westies had endeavored to sniff every square inch of pavement, and if her Westies had had a deep love for all things dirty.

"For example," I asked, "did you ever turn your head for a minute only to turn it back to find your dogs smearing the sides of their faces into something disgusting on the sidewalk?"

The answer to all my questions was yes.

The following June, we met Ian for the first time. Carlie has always been partial to her own breed, yet what I saw from her the day she first met Ian was a different level of exuberance.

Carlie has a variety of behaviors she displays when she is happy about something. Over the years, I have begun to think of these displays as Carlie's "dance moves." She stands firm on her paws and bites at the air and growls. I refer to this as the "Chomp-Chomp." She slides the side of her face along the ground with her rear in the air, while grunting. Because this puts me in mind of Arte Johnson's Renfield to George Hamilton's Dracula in the movie *Love at First Bite*, I call this move the "Renfield." She lies on her side and scissor-kicks her legs in the air: "Wild Thing." On the day she met Ian, Carlie broke out two of her three dance moves ("Chomp-Chomp" and "Renfield"), and then went running across an open stretch of lawn in the shape of a figure eight.

Ian, to his great credit, chomp-chomped right back at her,

and then he ran in a figure eight beside her. It was wonderful to watch. As they ran together that morning, the rational part of my mind explained this as fact: Westies prefer other Westies. The romantic part of my mind believed that Carlie and Ian, no fools they, recognized true love when they saw it.

Ian's person and I are of like minds: Dog walks in the park should not be planned like play dates, but rather should be fortuitous. Yet we began to meet every morning at the top of the Great Lawn. Ian, daring and adventurous, was the rough-and-tumble yin to Carlie's cautious and slightly goody-two-shoes yang. I soon found nothing quite so touching as when Carlie spied Ian across the Great Lawn and ran full speed ahead to meet him.

I learned that Ian's person was named Nancy. We began to joke that Carlie and Ian were very much in love. I didn't let on that I had suspected this all along. I suggested that since Carlie lives on the Upper East Side and Ian lives on the Upper West Side, they could be like a contemporary canine version of Mia Farrow and Woody Allen, only their cross-park love story would have within it a lot less crazy and a much happier ending.

Carlie and Ian meet most every morning in the park. Nancy and I have similar views on politics and books, and we talk about them while the dogs have a terrific run. One day I mentioned to Nancy that I was thinking of going to the Westminster Kennel Club show at Madison Square Garden.

"I'm going, too!" Nancy said. "Ian's breeder will be there. So will his sire."

I had sent Carlie's breeder an e-mail a few weeks earlier to compliment her on the Westie Christmas card (Carlie's *mishpokhe*, the lot of them, happy, bright-eyed, and beautiful) she sent me, and to inquire if she'd be at the dog show. She'd written back to say that she would not be attending, but that Carlie's father would be there, competing.

"Coincidence," I said to Nancy. "Carlie's father, sire, is going to be there, too."

Nancy mentioned how Ian's sire was coming all the way from Germany.

I stopped in my tracks. Germany?

I have a particular silly voice I use when I talk to Carlie. A lot of people do this with their dogs. I know it's not just me. "You're a Jersey girl," I sometimes say to her. It is, after all, true. Carlie hails from Cape May, New Jersey. "And you're half German," I'll say, because Carlie's father came over from Deutschland. (She's also a belly girl, but that's not so relevant to this story.)

"Carlie's father is from Germany!" I exclaimed, right there at the top of the Great Lawn, the place where I'd first heard about Ian, before he even *was* Ian.

"What's his name?" Nancy asked.

"I can get it off my e-mail at home," I said. "What's Ian's father's name?"

Nancy, too, had to look it up at home, though she did

have some recollection of it being fancy, and of course German.

"Yes," I agreed, "definitely fancy. And German."

"What are the chances?" we both wondered. As I watched Carlie and Ian run side by side up a hill, I observed how they looked *so alike*. They are both slightly on the small side. They are both more compact in body style than other Westies I have met. I remembered how both Carlie and Ian had hit their growth spurts at about a year and a half. Carlie's vet refers to this as the time that Carlie left her waistline behind.

*Could it really be?* As Carlie and Ian ran behind a tree, flipped over in tandem, and began rolling gleefully in whatever disgusting thing they had found there, their movements perfectly synchronized, the Central Park off-leash hours equivalent of a water ballet, I was sure I already knew the answer.

As soon as I got home from the park, I looked up the name of Carlie's father. It was German and fancy, and I e-mailed it to Nancy. Over the course of the afternoon, waiting for Nancy to reference the name of Ian's father and write back to me, I checked my e-mail much more than I usually do, and that's saying something. That evening I got an e-mail from her with the words, "It's official!" in the subject line. As I opened the message, my heart soared at the amazing coincidence of it all. Two Westies, one from Maryland and one from New Jersey, who shared a father and found each other by chance in Central Park.

Of course, the first to be told of this news was Carlie.

"You know Ian?" I said.

She gave a quick wag of her tail at the mention of Ian's name, once quickly to the left, once quickly to the right. I call this the "zoom zoom."

"He's not actually your boyfriend," I said, "he's your half brother!"

Carlie did look up at me, though she seemed unfazed, uninterested. Perhaps it was because this momentous news was delivered to her in the post-dinner hour, the time of day in which Carlie is least interested in the world around her. Of course, it could have been that, obviously, this was not news to Carlie. That this was something Carlie had known clearly, without any doubt, all along. And while this was the end of Carlie and Ian's great, though completely imagined romance, it was the beginning of what I think will prove to be one of my favorite happy coincidences.

I am not necessarily an eternal optimist. There are times when I think that New York City may in fact be a place that's almost too big for people to find the things for which they are looking. There are so many people here, so many humans off their leashes, how do you find anything? But if Carlie and Ian, two Westies, found each other in Central Park, it's hard not to believe that no matter how big a place, no matter how much distance must be covered in the search, it's entirely and wonderfully possible to find what you're looking for.

# 11

## Divorce Dogs

Keith and I had our first date on a Friday night in December, right in the middle of the first snowstorm of the year. Before our meeting, the things I knew about Keith were that he was divorced and his name was Keith. And he had two dogs.

This is why we were fixed up.

I looked forward to the date, and as I did I began to think that maybe someone like me will find happiness only with another dog person. The more I thought about it, the more I wondered how I'd ever seen it any other way, why I'd ever even bothered to accept a date from a man who didn't have a dog.

"He has those Chinese dogs," Jill, the friend who set us up, told me.

*Shar-Peis.* The words *cosmic* and *fated* ran through my mind. Upon hearing "those Chinese dogs," three little words I suddenly felt I'd been waiting my whole life to hear, it occurred to me, not for the first time, that Shar-Peis played a big part in making me who I am. I was, after all, raised side by side with an assembly of Chinese Shar-Peis! Spanky, the great canine love of my life (until I met Carlie), and whose picture still resides on the mantel of my fireplace, was a Shar-Pei. So when Jill said to me, "those Chinese dogs," I heard, "true love."

To add to my quite healthy nascent optimism about this blind date, Keith was very fond of his dogs. He mentioned them frequently (twelve times) in the three e-mails we exchanged before our date. In one, he wrote about the dogs being "powder puff." This made absolutely zero sense to me. I was unable to think of any aspect of a Shar-Pei's disposition, appearance, or behavior that could be described as "powder puff." It seemed off, incorrect, but I didn't inquire. Instead, I put the term *powder puff* entirely out of my mind. We were two people who were crazy about their dogs, and that was a good thing to have in common.

Keith and I met at a bar in the East Village that had old furniture upholstered in deep red, an old mahogany bar, and heavy red velvet drapes on the windows. He had dark hair and wore black-framed glasses. I thought he looked like Clark Kent or Peter Parker, though I wasn't sure which. I am aware that both Clark Kent and Peter Parker are comic book characters. Keith liked NPR, and, just as I did, he liked to listen to *This American Life* podcasts while on the treadmill. It was spectacularly hard to hear much of what Keith said over the din of the bar and the volume of the music. I found myself saying "Excuse me?" a lot more than a person normally says. Some things I just let go.

"The girls"—Keith's voice got louder, clearer; his words became more carefully enunciated—"love a bath!"

The topic of dogs and baths isn't one I often find the opportunity to participate in on dates, no matter how much I'd like to—so I began really focusing on what Keith was saying. Those words—*the girls love a bath!*—the way in which he said them, revealed a level of sensitivity, a certain compassion toward animals, that I had yet to come across in any of the men I had met in New York. I loved that he gave them baths. I loved that he took care of them. I loved that he called them "the girls"—such paternal sweetness. I'd finished my drink, and I noticed Keith was also done with his. He suggested we get dinner. We left the bar and headed out into the snowstorm.

As we walked to the restaurant that was closest, Keith commented on the fact that I am short. I recalled a time at a book party when I'd been introduced to a marketing executive from my publishing house. "Oh my God," she'd said, grabbing my hand and shaking it, "Alison Pace! I love your books!"

"Thank you," I'd said, genuinely pleased.

"I thought you'd be taller," she'd said next, and I hadn't known what to say other than "No, I'm not." I'd like to take a moment here to point out that Keith was not a tall man. (Nor was he exactly a slender man, but that's beside the point.)

At dinner, instead of dwelling on the height comment, I decided to talk about the dogs. "So, the girls," I began, embracing Keith's terminology, "I actually grew up with *three* Chinese Shar-Peis."

Keith looked confused. "I don't have Shar-Peis."

For a moment: disappointment. And then it hit me. When Jill had said "those Chinese dogs," she hadn't meant Shar-Peis, she'd meant the other kind of Chinese dogs. Pugs! Pugs were just as cosmic, and fated—I had written a novel about them.

"Oh, the girls are pugs?" I asked, smiling.

"No," Keith said again. "They're Chinese cresteds."

"The hairless dogs?" I asked. I took a deep breath. *Completely hairless but for one plume of hair, a crest if you will, on the top of their heads?* "With the crest on their head?" I added hastily, worried that calling them hairless could be considered rude.

"Yes," Keith said.

I sat, wordless. A distance sprang up between us I was unsure we'd cross.

"But there are two varieties. Hairless, which is what

114

you're thinking of," he explained. "Some of them, the ones with recessive genes, have hair. They're called powder puffs."

*Powder puff.*

"So, they have some hair?" I asked, to be sure, even though right then I had the distinct feeling that sureness was no longer part of the equation.

"Yes," he told me, and I found some comfort in that, the fact that there was some hair. In retrospect, however, I do sometimes wonder if the dogs having hair was not the initially positive piece of information I had thought it to be. I wonder if it would have all gone differently had they not had any hair at all.

"And they're pocket sized," he told me next. He provided this last bit of information with a level of enthusiasm on par with revealing that the girls had each scored perfect 1600s on their SATs. "Their names are Lumlina and Ludmilla."

I tried not to judge. Surely, there had to be some relevant and illuminating backstory. I tried not to think that it seemed unmanly for a forty-year-old man to have two pocket-sized Chinese cresteds (regardless of whether they had hair).

It turned out that the girls were a throwback to Keith's married days. He'd gotten custody of them in his divorce. They were his divorce dogs. In the way I conceived them, divorce dogs were not the same as a divorce car, the two-seater, often foreign sports car a divorced man in a movie drives so as not to feel emasculated by his marital shortcomings and in order to impress and possibly sign up new, shallow, and materialistic women who care about things like sports cars. I decided on the spot that these were dogs that the man himself had not chosen (and God willing had not named) but yet he loved them, and cared for them, and that made him a really nice person.

As we left the restaurant, Keith mentioned that he'd driven to the bar earlier and asked if I'd like a ride home. I accepted the ride. Coincidentally, or perhaps not so, Keith drove a divorce car.

In recounting the date, I told Jill how charming I found it that Keith referred to the dogs as "the girls."

On our second date the girls were mentioned a lot. I understood. Of course I understood! Did I not remember that time at a wedding, right after I'd gotten Carlie, and I was telling a fellow wedding guest all about her and he'd said to me, "Excuse me for one second, I'll be right back," and never came back? I remembered. And possibly because of that, I had a lovely time with Keith. He was smart. He was funny.

On our third date, we had dinner and then went back to Keith's apartment to meet the girls. They greeted us at the door. Their faces were in fact hairless, and their bodies were covered with long stringy hair. The hair, however, did not seem to be long for this world. It was falling from their bodies with each jerking movement they made. They had extremely long toenails, and as we walked into the apartment, I noticed that every surface was both scratched and covered in a thin layer of long, stringy, silvery dog hair. We sat on the couch with the girls. They were overjoyed to see Keith, climbing on him and jumping and issuing barks that sounded so much like seal calls, even as one of them reached out with her raptor claw and scratched me. I observed the completely unselfconscious abandon with which Keith allowed them to French-kiss him. I listened as he spoke to them in full-on baby talk. It was a grating and noxious baby talk.

*Do I talk to Carlie like that?* I looked at my lap. *Maybe on the rare occasion . . .*

I looked up as Ludmilla (or had it been Lumlina?) burped right at me. After she belched she made a smacking sound with her maw, as if to be sure she made the most of it. I looked away, down at my lap again. It was covered in dog hair. I looked in the direction of the pass-through kitchen. On the wall were three framed pictures: one of Lumlina, one of Ludmilla, a shot of them sneering together in the center, all of them professional shots set against a soft lavender background, a color choice I did not feel went a tremendously long way in terms of complementing their unique personalities. After a half hour of sitting on the hairy sofa, we took the dogs for a walk around the block. Keith pointed out to me that Lumlina was pooping out rope, a result of her swallowing her rope toys whole.

When I got home that night, Carlie sniffed me and looked at me with an accusatory expression that in my Carlie-to-English dictionary (yes, I know, I'm not normal either) translated to *Have you been with another?*

"It's not a problem," I assured her.

Only it was. It really was. As I went to sleep that night, I could think only of the girls. The next morning I called Jill.

"I know this might sound weird coming from me," I began, "but I find his obsession with the dogs a little off-putting."

"Yes, it does sound weird coming from you."

Jill, apparently more of a fan of Keith's than she had initially let on, suggested—with some snideness—that people in glass houses shouldn't throw stones.

I immediately wondered what Jill really thought about me. I asked questions I was not sure I wanted the answers to. *Did Jill think I was completely boundary free and obsessive about my dog? Did I talk in baby talk to Carlie in front of people?*

I called my friend Ellie. Ellie did not know Keith; she could be unbiased. I repeated the pertinent details. Ellie was appropriately off-put. "Look," she said, "nothing you've told me about Keith sounds all that appealing, but if there are some things you like about him, I'd go out with him one more time. Just to be sure."

I did. At the end of the evening, which had taken place a block away from Keith's apartment, we went to "see the girls." Being inside that apartment was tantamount to swimming in a sea of hair. I noticed that in addition to the three professional photos there were snapshots of the girls *everywhere*. Everywhere I turned I was confronted with pictures of the girls or the actual girls themselves. I have a lot of photos of Carlie, but I don't display *all* of them. As one of them began to hump my leg, it dawned on me that they would be perfectly cast as the pets of the outsider vampires on *True Blood*. And just to be clear, when I say *vampires*, I do not mean the nice, handsome kind of vampires who seem to wonder why we all can't just love one another, but rather the other kind of vampires who are mostly preoccupied with trying to kill people.

"I have to go," I said. "I need to walk Carlie."

"Okay," Keith said, from the dog-hairy couch, "we can come with you."

*No* would have been the right thing to say. But Keith, the girls, and I rode in a cab together all the way uptown to my apartment.

In retrospect, it is clear to me that we should have introduced our dogs to each other on neutral territory. For when Keith, the girls, and I walked into my apartment, Carlie freaked out. She freaked out to such a great extent, and there was such a high level of screeching and territorial peeing and all-around hysteria, that I am beyond convinced that when Carlie looked back on it later, she must have been very embarrassed. I left the living room to get paper towels and a bottle of Fantastik. Keith was sitting on my couch, the girls were cowering in the corner, and Carlie was prancing back and forth lengthwise across the room, apparently feeling she'd won the dominance battle that had just been waged. When I returned, this is what I said: "I have to go."

"Where do you have to go?" Keith asked.

I realized that no matter how foreign the scene in front of me seemed, I was already home. I took a long look at the girls. They were filthy. For an instant I wanted, more than anything else, to go back to that moment in the bar when Keith, against a dimly lit, red velvet background, had looked me in the eye and told me, "The girls love a bath." If the girls loved a bath so much, I wondered, why didn't they seem to have ever had one?

After Keith and the girls left, I noticed that there was hair everywhere. I vacuumed my rug, couch, and curtains and Swiffered my floors. I wielded my lint brush for days. No matter what I did, the girl hair was still everywhere.

Maybe two people who are both crazy about their dogs simply adds up to too much crazy. As I vacuumed, I wondered if it all would have turned out differently if Keith had had a more manly type of dog. A Labrador, or maybe a rough-and-tumble rescue mutt from the shelter, a dog that would do well on a hiking trip, look sharp in a station wagon, chase after a bird?

Keith called later in the week. I'd been hoping he wouldn't. I was hoping it would never get to the point where I'd have to explain that while I was entirely aware of the high, high level of irony of the situation, I couldn't deal with his dogs. That I found his level of obsession, for lack of any better word, disturbing.

I called Keith back. For several minutes he spoke to me about a Nylabone the girls were in the midst of sharing. He described this to me in great detail, in baby talk. Then he asked me if I was around that coming weekend.

I looked down at my sweater. I pulled a long, stringy silver hair off it and said that unfortunately I was busy. After I hung up the phone, I changed my sweater. I took Carlie's collar and leash out of the closet.

"Come on, Carlie," I said. "Let's go for a walk."

And I didn't say it in baby talk.

# 12

·········

# The Side View of a Smile

The letter began cordially, *Dear Ms. Pace.* It continued, *You recently had a breast imaging exam at our office. On this examination we identified a finding that warrants further evaluation.*

I put down the letter. I took a deep breath, picked it up, and continued reading. *This should not cause you undue concern or alarm but should be completed at your earliest convenience.*

"Undue concern, my ass," I said, and read on.

*Many women receiving our request to return are understandably concerned that we have found something suspicious. You should know that the vast majority of recall visits result in a benign diagnosis. Although you may consider calling your*

*doctor or our office for more information, we would discourage*
*this as neither your doctor nor we can be helpful to you until the*
*needed examination is completed on your return visit.*

I called my doctor.

My doctor said that she couldn't offer an opinion until
the needed examination was completed on my return visit.
But she'd had "a long talk" with the radiologist. The majority of what I gleaned from that conversation were the words
*baseline, dense, nodule, mass,* and *appearance.* All of these words
were applied to my left breast, which I suddenly thought felt
a little weird.

I would by most counts consider myself a fairly health-
conscious person. I exercise three to four times a week. I can
run round the Central Park reservoir with the best of them.
I practice yoga, though not as much as I should. I take my
vitamins. I eat fruits and vegetables. I try to avoid fried
foods. Child free, and in the position to set my own work
hours, I get about four hundred times more sleep than other
women my age. Other than self-inflicted, I don't have that
much extreme stress in my day-to-day life.

But in college and for several years after, I smoked cigarettes. I smoked constantly. I also believe I have leached far
more than my fair share of toxins out of plastic things over
the years, particularly Poland Spring water bottles. I have a
terrible habit of chewing on things: pen caps, little pieces of
paper I tear off pads and out of notebooks, and occasionally,

tape. Straws. And those little plastic rings that remain on the neck of the aforementioned Poland Spring water bottles once the cap has been removed. I have chewed them all in the throes of writing. I shuddered to think of all the possible carcinogens I had been pumping into my bloodstream. I cursed the thousands of sodium-laden and chemical-laced low-fat, low-calorie microwave dinners I had consumed over the years in the hope of losing the five to ten pounds I am, in perpetuity, trying to lose.

After phoning up my friends, and my ultimate authority on most subjects, my mother, I learned that this second test was not so unusual. Some women, including those on the maternal side of my family, have dense breast tissue, and sometimes a second test is necessary. It was nothing to worry about, my mother said. And then it was time to go back for the test. One of the radiologists appeared afterward and we reviewed my films together.

"See that, there." He pointed to a shadow. "That's what I was concerned about." I held my breath. "But I think you're just fine," he said.

And that was it. I went home and looked somewhat suspiciously at my newly purchased case of antioxidant-filled organic green tea.

Three weeks later I got a phone call from the radiologist's receptionist inquiring—*scolding* is another word—why I had not responded to the office's recently sent letter.

"Your health is a serious matter, not one that should be taken lightly."

"I got the letter and returned about three weeks ago," I explained.

But another letter had been sent. Though I was not in receipt of it, it said that my tests were once again concerning, and I needed to return for an ultrasound. The receptionist told me I needed to come back as soon as possible and gave me an appointment the following week.

"You know, this is why I hate managed care," my OB-GYN told me when I called her and discovered that the radiologist had not alerted her to this new development.

"Okay, at this point I'm concerned," my mother confided when I called.

"What's this doctor's last name?" my nana asked when she called.

"McKean," I told her. "Why?"

"You must have a Jewish doctor," Nana informed me. "The Gentiles don't know from medicine."

"As soon as the radiologist shows up, you know you're in trouble," said one of my friends who was not going to earn any gold stars in sensitivity.

For someone never very interested in the phone, answering it, talking on it, I was suddenly quite into it. I called a few more friends. Each one of them asked when and where the third appointment was, and if I wanted her to come with me. I thought taking any of them up on it would be making too much of a big deal. Instead, I became obsessed with my neighbor's cigarette smoking. I was convinced that his secondhand smoke was the root of all evil. My neighbor and I share a bathroom wall and I was convinced that the smoke was getting into my apartment not only through the front door (it got in that way, too) but through the drain in the shower and the sink. I bought rubber drain stoppers for both of our shower drains. Because I had, in more carefree times, occasionally gone next door to smoke one of my neighbor's cigarettes, my frosty presentation of the drain stoppers caused him to inquire why he was living in a Fellini movie.

I remain unsure as to whether he ever embraced his drain stopper, but I focused my attention on smoke that got in through the front of the apartment. My neighbor was a nice friend and on occasion a confidant. We order Indian food together on the random Sunday night. He makes juice for me in the Jack LaLanne juicer he received one year for Christmas. He'll make me an espresso in his espresso machine if I e-mail ahead. If I bring my own milk, he'll make it a latte. For the week leading up to my third mammogram, I hated him.

My mother suggested I get a draft dodger for my front door. "They're nice; they look just like a stuffed snake."

I bought one. It would look even more like a snake were I to draw an eye and a smile on it. But I did not. Instead, I barricaded myself into my hermetically sealed apartment, and as the third visit to the radiologist approached, it occurred to me that this was it: The terrible thing we all secretly fear might happen had, in fact, happened.

The day before the third test, I slept late. I took my dog for a longer walk in the park than usual. I ran on the treadmill at the gym, something that, along with stopping by the vegan restaurant on my block for a large shot of wheatgrass, I had done every day that week. After the gym, I stopped by my friend Sarah's apartment for lunch. She was busy on WebMD, trying to diagnose herself with celiac disease.

I returned to the radiologist not filled with (but aware of) a sense of dread. This time I went to a different floor, the ultrasound floor. In the waiting room, I noticed a woman, maybe a few years older than me, waiting with her mother. They looked so much alike, there wasn't any doubt it was her mother. I was struck with the thought that it was possible that I would never take my mother to her doctor's appointments when she was older. Not that this is something I've ever planned for enthusiastically, but it's the natural order of things. I realized then how possible it is that the natural order of things can be all wrong.

I worried about my dog. Who would take Carlie?

I had an ultrasound. The radiologist, a different radiologist, introduced herself by way of saying, "I heard you kind of slipped through the cracks." I wondered if she was the previous radiologist's superior, or just another radiologist. I wondered if she was Jewish. Later, after I had another mammogram, this new radiologist and I reviewed all the results together.

She pointed to something on the film. "That was what I'd been nervous about, but I'm not nervous anymore." I was fine, she said.

"Completely fine?" I asked. I felt at this point it was better to double-check than to continue on with this office in the role of the perpetual pen pal who never has the opportunity to write back.

"Absolutely fine," she confirmed. "But you should come back in six months for another mammogram. Just to be safe," she added, so that while I felt tremendous relief there remained a kernel of fear.

I walked downstairs. I stood in the lobby. I took out my phone, because after the great angst, I didn't want to shed tears of relief in the street. It has been my experience that crying on the streets of New York City (and I'd imagine the streets of any city, though I myself only have experience with New York City) makes you look like a crazy person. I called my parents first and told my mom I was fine, nothing at all to worry about. She said she'd been sure all along that would be the case. As soon as I knew I was safe from any emotional outburst, I headed out to the street.

"Well," my mom said next, "now that that's behind us, we have sad news."

I stopped walking.

Mom told me that one of their dogs, Dunner, a Boston

terrier who'd been dearly loved in spite of his incontinence, had passed away. At the corner of Eighty-fourth Street and Lexington Avenue, I burst into tears.

This all happened right before the holidays, right before New Year's. My resolution, along with lose five pounds, don't stay in exercise clothes all day every day especially when I have no intention of exercising, stop eating paper and chewing on plastic, and at least consider answering the phone when it rings, was to think less about the bad things and more about the good things. I try to stick to it. A year, even a day before this happened, I would not have guessed that my current version of "raindrops on roses and whiskers on kittens" in its own circuitous way includes two mammograms and an ultrasound. But when I fall into a rut or forget for a moment that there is a tremendous amount to be thankful for, when I think about the things I don't have, I stop and think about two mammograms and an ultrasound. And then I don't dwell so much on the things I don't have. I think about the things that I do. Among many other things, I have a door snake, upon which I have drawn the side view of a smile.

# 13

## Dog Gone

I met Stuart at a work party, a networking thing. I thought it was nice that he had crossed the room to talk to me. I had concerns that he might be five to ten years younger than me, but when he laughed his teeth were endearingly crooked. The things Stuart said were funny. Then Stuart revealed that he'd be turning forty in a few weeks, which made him five years older than me. He gave me his business card and asked me for mine.

"I'd really like to get in touch with you," he said, quite charmingly.

In lieu of a business card, I peeled off the name tag I'd worn because of the nature of the event and handed it to him.

Stuart smiled as he folded my name tag in half and put it in his pocket. He told me that he thought that I was, and I quote, "made of awesome."

He e-mailed me the next day and asked me out for the upcoming weekend. We had our first date on the Sunday night of Memorial Day weekend. Though three-day weekends for the most part mean nothing to me in terms of work—my writing schedule veers between being always at my desk for days on end to being physically unable to sit at it for longer than thirty minutes—I love New York best on holiday weekends. The city is quiet, it's easy to get a dinner reservation, and there are half as many people everywhere. A friend told me once that she felt a little bit left out being in New York on a holiday weekend. Yes, but it's the very best kind of left out.

That night, Stuart and I met at a Starbucks near the Seventy-seventh Street subway station and headed out into one hundred percent humidity (and the threat of impending rain) for a stroll in Central Park. Once there, Stuart suggested a drink, and I suggested the Boat House. As we crossed the street, Stuart pointed out an approaching dog.

"Look, it's a pug," he said, nudging my arm and pointing.

"That's a French bulldog," I corrected. Then I added, "But you were close, they both have snub noses."

"You know a lot about dogs," he said. I did not get the impression he meant this as a compliment.

We arrived at the Boat House and secured a good table right next to the lake. I ordered a glass of wine and Stuart ordered a beer. Stuart told me about the years he'd spent living in Seattle and how one of the things he'd liked about that city was the many opportunities it afforded the camping enthusiast.

"I've never been to Seattle. I've always wanted to go," I said. I went on to elaborate that I felt I had a very outdoorsy side to my personality that, living in New York as I did, I didn't get to explore nearly enough.

This was both true and not true. I wanted to seem like his type.

Stuart nodded keenly. "There are great places to go camping outside New York."

"How terrific!" I said. To further highlight the outdoorsy side of myself, I revealed that I had written a magazine article on adventure travel with your dog. I did not mention that because of budgetary constraints, it was not so much "adventure travel" as two afternoon hikes. "I bought a special safety hiking harness for Carlie. It literally turned her into a four-legged Samsonite so I could lift her up and over obstacles."

Stuart blinked more times than could be considered necessary. And then he changed the subject. We went to dinner, and by the time I got home we'd had a six-hour date. I went to sleep thinking there would definitely be a second date. On Monday, Stuart e-mailed and we made a date for Thursday and proceeded to spend the remaining three days in the throes of full-on e-mail banter.

As we settled into bar stools on our second date, we began

by talking about our days. Stuart had given a pitch, one that everyone loved. It was, he said, "a moment."

I liked that he called it a moment. I am a fan of the moment.

"Working from home, by yourself, is there an equivalent of nailing a presentation?"

Right then, rainy air blew in at me from the entrance of the bar. "No," I said, "I don't think there really are any."

"That's too bad," he said.

I felt irritated. "There are other triumphs," I said.

Stuart changed the subject. "Well, you said you liked camping," he began, "and I'm going this weekend with friends. I was wondering if you'd like to come with us? It's just a quick overnight. We're leaving Saturday morning and coming back Sunday morning."

"Yes," I said. "I'd love to come." I said it simply and straightforwardly. I didn't hem or haw, and I didn't worry about sleeping arrangements, or expectations, or what the friends would be like. I wanted to go, so I said yes.

"You know, I don't want you to think I'm asking you to go away for the weekend with me after only two dates," he said next.

"No," I said, "of course not."

"You don't think it's too much?" he asked. I found his insecurity charming. "Because," he continued, "our first date was, what, seven hours long, so it really counts as two dates. So this, technically, is our third date, and"—he looked down with a flourish at his watch—"who knows, it could also wind up counting as two."

I do at this juncture fully admit that just as I had not thought twice about going off into the woods with a person I had not yet known for a total of twelve hours, I did not think twice about my next question.

"Is it okay with you if I bring my dog?"

My dog is, without question, a country dog who happens to live in the city. I try to make this up to her as best as I can. I am diligent about getting her to the park every morning for off-leash hours. On spring and summer weekends, I pack up a blanket and a book and her portable water dish and return to the park for a few hours more. I take her to the beach with me whenever I go.

"Sure," he said. In the moment after I asked that question, there was a skip, a shift, an almost imperceptible but wholly relevant change that came over us, not unlike the moment when PMS symptoms transition from bitchiness to despair. Yet (incredible as it seems to me now) as the night came to an end, I had nothing but optimism about the upcoming camping trip.

By the time I woke up on Friday morning, I was looking forward to it even more. I located my sunscreen. I retrieved my hiking boots from where they'd been long stowed, far under the bed. I pulled my sleeping bag, unused since the great white-water rafting expedition of '01, out of the closet and stopped by the vet's office to get Carlie a Preventic tick collar.

The e-mail from Stuart arrived at four in the afternoon. He expressed envy at the fact that I was able to work from home and shared that he himself was "hitting the wall." He went on to say that he'd given it some thought and since I had to be back in the city on Sunday and it was no fun to get up early to take down the tent and there might be traffic and he didn't want either of us to be stressed maybe this weekend camping wouldn't make the most sense.

And, new sentence, he worried there might be rain in the forecast.

Because of a complete lack of punctuation, I had to read the e-mail twice.

My first thought upon completion was that I was at a loss for what had transpired, post-invite. Then I considered that maybe Stuart was a jackass. And then I thought that I'd actually been looking forward to going camping with him.

I wrote back, breezy, that *all* those reasons made sense and I hoped he had a nice weekend. When no return e-mail was forthcoming, I knew. I knew the way you know it's about to rain. I just didn't know why.

Sunday, at six exactly, Stuart e-mailed again.

Hey.

After some thinking, I've decided that I'm going to have to go with the late-thirties dating logic we were talking about and say that since you're not 100% perfect for me we both know it's better to end things now rather than later. And I think you need someone who will jump at the chance to road trip with your dog rather than go through a long list of hesitations.

Stuart

I wanted to point out that I did not remember any conversation about "the late-thirties dating logic," and that while we were on the subject, I was still in my *mid*thirties, and he was going to be forty in about a minute. But I did not. There is nothing good about it when someone takes it upon himself to point out to you that, in his opinion, you're not actually that awesome after all.

I read the e-mail over again.

I forwarded the e-mail to my friend Robin. I also forwarded it to my mother (though only to disprove her theory that I was single because I'm too picky). Robin advised me to throw him in the jackass bin and close the lid tight. My mother gently pointed out that perhaps this might have had something to do with Carlie.

"I can't *imagine* it had anything to do with that," I said.

Mom assured me that it did. She suggested I send him a photo of Carlie. She then relayed a recent conversation she'd had with my aunt, who had pointed out that it's much harder for people in their thirties to meet people than it is for people in their twenties. That part of the conversation did not go particularly well.

Because I am afflicted with a condition that makes it almost impossible for me to not respond to an e-mail message, I sat down at my desk. Not responding would convey a level of woundedness that I was not at all prepared to own. I sought to strike the right balance between *That's fine* and *If this is about my dog, you're kind of a dick*. I composed an e-mail. And deleted it. I composed another and deleted it as well.

A few minutes later, my neighbor rang my doorbell, asking if I'd like to come over and have a glass of wine with him, his new girlfriend, and his visiting cousin. I did. It was not my desire to be a self-centered ninny and monopolize the conversation with my most recent tale of dating woe, but we all have our moments, and this was one of mine. I relayed the story to my neighbor and he said it was definitely about my dog. His girlfriend agreed.

"That makes the guy a douche bag," she said.

I've never liked the term *douche bag*, but right then I loved it. The visiting cousin agreed that it was absolutely about my dog, even though he thought my dog (who had come next door with me, no problem) was extraordinarily cute. I noticed the visiting cousin had nice teeth.

"You're really upset, aren't you?" my neighbor said.

I admitted that I was, more so than I thought I should be. Two dates with someone does not an investment make, but still.

My neighbor's new girlfriend asked, "Did you write back?"

I said I hadn't yet.

She suggested: *Dear Douche Bag, I completely agree.*

I liked that, and stealing the idea from my mother without giving her any credit said, "Yes, that or send him a picture of my dog."

It was then that the idea struck us all at once. We made a night of it. We ordered in Indian food and we made a sign that said "I AGREE." In bold letters inside a speech bubble. I loved the artfully placed period most of all. We styled Carlie, we arranged her on the couch with the sign in front of her, and my neighbor, an excellent photographer, took a round of shots with one of those very big and important-looking cameras. We settled on one in which the lighting was ideal and the look on Carlie's face was a perfect mixture of confusion and disdain.

In my life there have been e-mails I have sent that I have later come to regret. This is one of them. I sent the picture to Stuart.

What I didn't immediately admit to myself was this: I had finally become a crazy dog lady.

# 14

## Therapy Dogs

Most days, Carlie and I leave the apartment somewhere between quarter to eight and eight in the morning. This gives us enough time to walk the four long, filled-with-myriad-things-to-sniff crosstown blocks (it takes longer than you'd think) to Central Park, where we then either walk the loop around the Great Lawn or play fetch for a while before the officially designated nine o'clock end of off-leash hours.

Some days, though, days on which I don't really have any better excuse than getting a late start, we head out to the park a bit later. I'd say at around nine thirty. I've determined that if you're going to be renegade and let your dog off her leash past the end of off-leash hours (and I'll admit, I'm a bit of a renegade), the block of time between nine and nine thirty is the most dangerous. After that, you can get away with things.

On these late days, Carlie and I walk the loop of the Great Lawn in comparative solitude. The great majority of dogs have left the park, and the ones that remain are on their leashes. Carlie is sometimes on her leash, too. Sometimes she is not. I worry about writing that down. I worry that the wrong people will read it and before I know it, the NYPD will have an all-points bulletin out every morning for a rebel unleashed Westie.

There was one summer, what we might call a between-books summer, in which there was a greater frequency of late starts out to the park. One of the things that became memorable about the late-start mornings that summer was that on those days, right at the northernmost edge of the Great Lawn, a place close to the spot where Carlie and I first heard about Ian and later met him, we would run into another Westie. His name was Simba.

As I'm sure I have by now made clear, Carlie is particularly fond of her fellow Westie. Simba was no exception. She became instantly thrilled on the mornings we ran into him, and in the rare event she wasn't already off her leash when we saw him, I let her off. At first sight, they ran to each other around the curve of the Great Lawn, a definite air of "Born Free" to it. They did the usual Westie things, the chomp-chomp, the spinning, the quick stop/pivot/run quickly in the other direction that was Carlie's favorite. They were mirror images of each other. I looked on, as proud and pleased at the sight of Carlie's happiness as I was that first time she ate out of her bowl, the first day she was in my apartment. Carlie seemed to enjoy Simba so much, as much as if not more than she enjoyed running into Ian when we left the house earlier, that it was almost an excuse to linger in, just to arrive at the park late.

As has been my predominant experience with dog people in Central Park or elsewhere, the first one or two times Carlie and Simba met, the conversation I had with the person on the other end of Simba's leash (or letting go of Simba's leash as the case may have been) was limited to "Hi" and "What's your dog's name?" On the second meeting, I commented to Simba's person, a nice woman a few years older than me who had a gentle, pleasant, and laid-back manner, that he and Carlie looked so much alike.

"They do, don't they?" she agreed, and I wondered, could it be, another of the brethren of Carlie and Ian in Central Park? (It wasn't.) A few meetings later, after a few more conversations that consisted almost solely of "Aren't they adorable," "Westies are such a great breed," "Westies are so smart and so sweet," and "I love Westies," we exchanged names. Hers: Sherry.

A few visits in, Sherry took out her phone and snapped a picture of our two dogs playing together. She leaned her BlackBerry in my direction to show off the cuteness of the snap of the two dogs running toward us. In my mind there are few things more charming than a Westie running straight at you.

"Oh," I remarked, ever of the belief that there is never such a thing as too many cute pictures of my dog. "I'd love a copy."

"Sure," Sherry said. She typed as I spelled out my e-mail address to her, and I watched as she hit send. "Thanks," I added as she put away her phone. "I can't wait to see it on-screen when I get home."

The first thing I did when I got home that morning was look at my e-mail for the picture of Simba and Carlie. As I saved the snap to iPhoto, I noticed that the signature on Sherry's e-mail included Sherry's first and last name, followed by Ph.D., followed by an office address just off Park Avenue, a suite on the first floor. I don't think I thought much about it then—at least not on a conscious level, as Freud would say—but I did think, *Oh, that nice lady in the park with the Westie must be a therapist.* Soon after, I suggested a book to Sherry. My book, the one that features a Westie named Carlie. I mean, when it came to the Westie, Sherry was clearly a fan. People get that way over their chosen dog breeds. I think with any breed, there's a lot of breed loyalty, a camaraderie, a sense that someone else who has the same breed as you knows the exact same secret handshake. It's certainly true with Westies.

"You know, if you like Westies, you might like my book,"

I offered, and Sherry immediately asked me the title. *"City Dog,"* I told her, adding that there was a picture of a Westie, not actually Carlie, on the cover of the book. The dog, I elaborated, lest she miss it, is standing on top of a taxicab. "This is perfect," Sherry told me, explaining that she was about to leave for a two-week trip and needed some reading material. I smiled; I was happy at this news and told her so.

A few weeks later, a few weeks in which the warm summer weather and a stretch of sun-filled days had jarred me right out of my late-start rut, and Carlie and I had been early each day to the park, and we hadn't seen Simba and Sherry again, an e-mail arrived from Sherry. It was titled, I thought perfectly, *Loved the Book!* She wrote: *I'm so glad I brought* City Dog *on my trip with me. It was just delightful, in so many ways, on so many different levels.*

She went on to say that though she didn't know how close the book hit home for me, she thought I captured perfectly what she—and so many other divorced women in New York City—go through. That part gave me an extra sense of pride, knowing that I, never having been a divorced woman, had gotten that element of my character right. She said I nailed the Westie mannerisms right on the head. That part I already knew, but it was, as praise always is, nice to read. Her note was well written and thoughtful. It had the perfect number of exclamation points, along with a promise to pick up the other books I had written. It was the fan letter every writer hopes to get. At the end, she mentioned how she'd just gotten back from a weekend away and was anxiously awaiting Simba's return from his dog walker, who'd had him all weekend.

Oh, I thought, I knew the feeling. No matter where I went, or whom I was with, I missed Carlie a lot when I traveled without her. And also, there is nothing quite like a welcome home from a dog. I wrote back, thanking her profusely for the good words about the book, and sent Carlie's regards to Simba.

We saw Sherry and Simba only one more time that summer. As Carlie ran up to Simba, stopped short in front of him, pivoted around, and ran quickly in the opposite direction, and Simba gave chase, I thanked Sherry again for her e-mail.

"I noticed on your e-mail signature that you're a Ph.D., so you're a therapist?" I asked.

"Yes," she told me. "We live on the west side but our office is over on the east, so we do this walk every day before our first appointment."

"And Simba comes with you?" I asked. I loved that. I loved jobs where people could bring their dogs to work with them. It's up there as one of my favorite things about being a writer.

"Yes," Sherry said, her gaze following Simba as he ran from Carlie. "He comes with me."

I remembered a brief time I had spent years earlier with a therapist named Lois. She had a Portuguese water dog, Flora. They had the same setup. Lois and Flora lived on the Upper West Side, the traditional home of New York City therapists, but Lois had her practice on the Upper East Side, too. I liked Flora. She was for the most part catatonic and spent the majority of her time in repose in a plaid dog bed in the corner, raising her head in greeting when I arrived. Once she came and sat next to me.

Lois had told me that Flora sometimes worked with patients, and though I had wondered why she never worked with me, I never inquired. Once Lois told me to imagine that all my negative feelings, along with my critical inner voice, were an actual black swirling monster in the corner of any room I happened to be in. I remember how she told me that the better I was able to visualize the black swirling monster, the better I'd be able to keep any negative thoughts and emotions in my life at bay. I had not been good at envisioning the black swirling monster. It occurs to me now that for Lois's patients who didn't really like dogs maybe Flora, black but not really swirling, had been helpful for some with that visualization.

When I switched insurance carriers to a plan Lois wasn't on, she informed me that she thought I'd done all the work I'd needed to do. In the way that I once put off breaking up with a guy for much longer than I should have because I was in love with his dog, a beautiful white-and-tan shepherd mix named Kevin with one ear that stood up and one that flopped down, my initial thought after this announcement had been about Flora. Innocuous though she had been, my first thought was that I was going to miss seeing her.

"Does Simba ever work with your patients?" I asked Sherry.

"Mmm," Sherry considered this. "I don't really think so. Though sometimes they hold him, so I think that could count."

"That's cute that they hold him," I said. We watched our dogs as they ran in a circle around us. There was something in Carlie and Simba's movements and the expressions on both their faces that reminded me of the cartoon characters Pepé Le Pew and Penelope Pussycat, only the traditional gender roles were reversed and Carlie appeared to be the one greatly more pursuant of *l'amour*.

That summer passed and most of that fall did, too. It was right after Thanksgiving and I was in the midst of experiencing a one-two punch of professional and personal dismay. I was having, as they say, a rough time. One morning, walking around the loop of the Great Lawn, I found myself wondering if we'd see Sherry and Simba, because it was late. I didn't see them anywhere, not on the lawn or on the approach from the west. My first thought was that maybe it wasn't late enough. And then, one of those blips from the past, a snapshot: I recalled a conversation I'd been part of once about someone starting therapy in his sixties. Someone had inquired, "Isn't that kind of late?" "No, no," someone else had answered. "It's never too late."

I stopped walking to wait as Carlie sniffed at some tree. It was one of those cold, dreary December days when there is no sunlight at all, only gray and too much wind. I looked at the already bare treetops and I thought that it wasn't really a matter of our being too late to see Sherry and Simba, but rather a matter of realizing it was never too late.

I went home. I searched my in-box to find the summer e-mail from Sherry. I did so by searching for *Simba*. I sent one back. I titled it "inquiry." I acknowledged that this was not the most traditional way of finding a therapist and asked if she took Empire.

I turned from my e-mail and wondered if she was even accepting new patients. A lot of therapists in New York aren't.

I checked my e-mail. Sherry had written back. In a font that wasn't your standard e-mail Arial, but still something from the sans serif family, and in a deep blue hue, she wrote: *Hi, Alison, it's good to hear from you. You're right, it's not the most traditional way of finding a therapist, but sometimes non traditional things work for the best.* She suggested I call her office to talk about it on the phone. She signed off by saying that she hoped Carlie and I were enjoying the beautiful weather. I wasn't sure what she meant by that, as I was certain that the day outside was overcast and gray.

Sherry and I talked on the phone. We sorted out details pertaining to insurance, and I scheduled my first appointment and she gave me her address. I knew the block well, could picture the frame shop on the corner and the way that once you turned off the avenue there was a direct line of sight to the entrance of the Metropolitan Museum of Art: my favorite view in New York.

As Sherry and I made these plans, as I jotted the possibly fortuitous address on a pad, I thought of a writing teacher I'd had once who'd said she had always brought her dog with her to therapy. At the time it had sounded strange to bring a dog to therapy. I had also understood it, deeply, on a level I hadn't yet accessed. I wondered, in the moments before Sherry and I hung up, if I could bring Carlie with me. I didn't ask.

Instead, I hung up the phone and thought, *I'm going back to therapy.* I thought that it was possible that Lois had been wrong when she'd declared me "done." I thought it possible that the therapist before her, one I'd seen in my twenties, had been right when he'd told me that I had a lot more work left to do, immediately after my announcement that I didn't see therapy as a part of my future. In my defense, his main insight had been that I had a complicated relationship with food, and really, who doesn't?

I picked the phone back up and called my mother. This is pretty much my reaction to all events in my life, major, minor, and all those many filler moments in between: I call my mom.

"Hi, Mom," I said, and after the usual greetings, an inquiry on my end after Bailey and Jessica, and of course, my dad, and an inquiry on her end after Carlie, I shared my most recent news. "I've decided to go back to therapy," I announced. "What do you think?"

My mom hesitated. Coming from anyone, "What do you think about my going to therapy?" is a loaded question. An answer of "Yes, I think you've made a good decision there" cannot be uttered without a truckload of subtext.

Much more weightily, this was a question posed by a daughter to a mother. In my conversations with friends and others who have undergone therapy, two things have jumped out at me: People tend to spend the first few sessions crying, and at one point or another, they find themselves upset with their mothers.

My mom knew this. My mom has a master's degree in psychology. My aunt and uncle are both psychologists. My sister went to graduate school for social work. At our family holidays, you can't throw a rock without hitting someone studied in the field. My mom knew better than most people that therapy equals a skip down a (not necessarily rose-petal-strewn) memory lane called Mom.

"If you think it's going to help," she said, "then by all means you should go."

I went. The following week, I walked the seven blocks north to Sherry's office. And I spent the entire first session in tears, at the end of which I asked if next time I could bring my dog. Sherry said yes. She added that she was sure Simba would be happy to see her.

And so Carlie started going to therapy.

She was remarkably (perhaps a little distressingly) indifferent to any crying. She was much more interested in taking every one of Simba's plentiful small stuffed toys out of his bed one by one and shaking them back and forth as if they were real, live vermin in need of being killed dead. Simba looked on in what I was pretty sure was horror. But still, in the way my writing teacher of years ago had said it could be, I found it both helpful and comforting at once to have her there.

It was also fun. The glee that would fill Carlie's eyes when four o'clock on Wednesdays would roll around and I'd say to her, "What do you think, do you want to go see Simba?" was so apparent and, to me, priceless. She would run to the front door and jump on it. She pranced to the elevator, out of the building, and all the way up Third Avenue. In my earlier forays into therapy, I'd had a propensity to be flaky. I'd cancel appointments at the last minute. I made excuses. There were so many weeks that I just couldn't wrap my head around the thought of it, and I'd convince myself that I was more than happy to pay for not going. But with Sherry that never happened. I never canceled, never missed. On Wednesday afternoons, Carlie would dash up Third Avenue. She would turn and charge toward Park Avenue, and turn right into Sherry's building, filled with a speed I rarely saw and a purpose and determination I often did.

Simba would always greet us at the door, though I believe he looked at Carlie with slight trepidation. Almost out of a sense of obligation, it seemed, he'd chase her in a quick figure eight once or twice around the room, and then retire to his chair where he watched with bemused fascination as she waged her weekly assault against his stuffed toys.

There were times when I looked forward to therapy, times when I was having a particular issue with family or work or friends and needed a sounding board. There were far more times when I didn't look forward to therapy at all, but I told myself I could go for Carlie. Caring for Carlie, being responsible for her meals, walks, safety, health, and happiness, had introduced me to a level of commitment I hadn't yet experienced with another being. It's possible that the joy Carlie got from her weekly visits to Sherry's office introduced me to a level of commitment to therapy I'd never had.

While the Carlie parts of therapy were fun—the walks there, the Westie chase, the piece of string cheese that Sherry would split between the two dogs as they sat, identical reflections of each other, waiting for her to get the plastic wrap off—there were a lot of other parts of therapy that were not. I've now accepted and even embraced the fact that therapy, if you're doing it right, if you're really (to use a bit of therapy-speak here) putting the work in, can be awful. I had to look at things I didn't want to look at. I cried a lot. I was pissed at my mother. But also, I started to realize over the course of many months that I was the common denominator in a lot of the problems in my life. It occurred to me—slowly, and sort of horribly—that in many scenarios, it hadn't been *everyone else*. It had been me.

It was rough. But anyone will tell you that it's not supposed to be easy.

I stuck with it, maybe a little bit because of the doggie play date aspect of it, and because I was ready to. I thought of what my mom had said: *If you think it's going to help, then by all means you should go.* It helped. It was helping.

And then Sherry informed me that she'd be moving offices. She would, within a matter of weeks, be leaving the lovely parlor floor suite right off Lexington Avenue and heading over to the Upper West Side. High up on the Upper West Side. It was a trip that would take two buses and about forty minutes each way for every fifty-minute session. In order for Carlie to come, she'd have to be stuffed into her Sherpa bag, which she had since outgrown. And even if she hadn't, she hates that bag. Upon sight of it she cries, her ears go flat back as does her tail, and she runs from the room and hides. I have no idea what puppyhood trauma Carlie associates with her travel bag, but I believe it to be significant. The few times when a bagged Carlie has been unavoidable, it has been followed by doggie vomit and diarrhea.

I switched my weekly appointment to nine thirty on Tuesdays. This way, I reasoned, I could simply extend the morning dog walk northward and westward a bit, and we'd walk to therapy and then back. Yes, it would add an hour or two to the morning routine, but I figured it would work.

It was not, in the end, the easiest transition. I have learned in life that many transitions are not. This particular shift took place in the midst of a hot New York City summer, and Carlie, understandably, is not a fan of walking long distances in really hot weather. And I never loved sitting in therapy as sweaty as I would generally be after our crosspark journey. Also, Sherry's new office was a fair amount smaller than her previous one. It did not provide the space needed for the forging of a figure-eight-shaped track. This didn't seem to faze Carlie; she'd run up to Simba and stop short in front of him and then run in the other direction, occasionally into a wall.

Simba ignored Carlie, and often he'd wedge himself out of sight underneath a chair. Carlie looked from Sherry to me with an expression of grave concern. She sat in front of the chair that Simba had wedged himself underneath and made moany noises and, worse yet, sometimes cried.

A lot of what I've worked on in therapy has involved relationships, sorting them out, becoming better at identifying the bad ones. When I saw Carlie like that, pining after Simba, a door that simply wasn't going to open, and perhaps needed to be left shut, I knew that what Carlie needed to do was to recognize that fact and move on.

Briefly, I wondered whether it was possible that the Westies had discussed it among themselves and played this out for my benefit—canine therapy theater.

Simba had a problem with his hip, and had surgery, and was soon undergoing his own therapy. (Sherry sent me a video that Simba's physical therapist had posted on YouTube. In it, an earnest and focused Simba is submerged up to his neck in water and walking on a treadmill. It's adorable.) Since he needed his rest, Carlie needed to stay at home. And after that, I never really got back into the habit of bringing her.

For a while, I tried to replace this weekly event in Carlie's calendar with the "Yappy Hour" that takes place at the doggie day care down the street from my apartment, but Carlie never really seemed into it. She would spend most of the hour sitting up on a very dog-hair-covered couch, right next to me. As I was casting around for other ideas, I received an e-mail from Therapy Dogs, a group that trains dogs who visit sick people in hospitals and the elderly in nursing homes, or sit patiently and listen while learning-disabled children read to them. It was an organization I'd heard about, and I'd always been meaning to sign Carlie up. I read the e-mail and thought, *Of course, now is the time that I'll get around to it.* I was, after all, *evolving.*

The first step was to fill out an online questionnaire. I clicked right on over. I breezed through the initial questions: *How old is your dog? How long have you had your dog? Have you and your dog worked with a trainer? Taken obedience classes?*

Four. Three years. Yes. Yes.

*Can your dog do the following on command: Sit. Stay. Down?*

Yes, yes, yes! I answered. Even though the truth was more a maybe/depends.

There were more questions: *How does your dog do with other dogs/with loud noises/with people grabbing her/fireworks, thunderstorms?*

I answered these more honestly: sometimes she's fine/ sometimes she's scared/she's scared/she doesn't like it/she flips out. I used the extra space provided to elaborate on what I predicted would be Carlie's varied and nuanced reactions to the aforementioned situations. I noted our preferred placement (Carlie listening while learning-disabled children read to her) and hit send on our application.

A few days later I got an e-mail from the director of field operations for the organization. She wrote, in brief, that while Carlie seemed very sweet, she might not be a perfect fit for the program, as they needed dogs who were extremely confident. I would not describe Carlie as such. I replied truthfully, admitting that as I had been filling out the form I had begun to wonder if it was not the right fit for Carlie. I elaborated. *She's very smart and nice,* I began. *But she is definitely shy and some might say skittish with certain people. She appears, moreso than other dogs I've known, very concerned for her safety and well-being. I worry a little she might be too anxious and/or sensitive. As I got her when she was a year old, I'm not really sure what happened to her before I knew her, but she's not the most secure.*

The director wrote back that day to say that Carlie was lucky to have such a dedicated and caring owner, and I felt pride at that. We decided that maybe being a therapy dog might not be best for Carlie right then, but perhaps it was something that we could revisit when she got older. We signed off and the e-mails on the topic disappeared into the vortex of my sent mailbox. A year or so later, when I was searching for something else, I came across that e-mail I'd sent describing Carlie. After all that time, I was able to see that I could just as easily have been writing about myself.

I've read many romantic novels featuring dogs, and I have picked up on a common thread: There is often a scene in which the dog will lead the heroine to the thing she's been looking for all along: in many cases, a man. I've written scenes like this myself, without irony, with a completely straight face. My favorite is not one I wrote, however, but one I read in which the dog led the heroine to a man . . . but it turned out it was because the man was a butcher and smelled like meat.

I still have this romantic vision that one day Carlie will somehow be instrumental in helping me find love. She'll stop on a street corner to smell something and linger for a bit longer than necessary, and then, there, he'll crash right into us. But my romantic notions are not limited to future events. I believe it's already happened. Yes, I believe that me finding a therapist who worked for me had a lot to do with timing and as much to do with the idea that when you're ready for things you'll find them. I also believe that Carlie headed out into Central Park with a purpose and found me something that I needed.

# 15

## On Bright Green Shirts and Jack Russell Terriers

I was visiting Long Island a few Februarys ago and my mom and I were sitting in the den in front of a fire. We sat there with Carlie and with what we referred to, fondly if a bit wistfully, as the geriatric crew. My parents' two current dogs—Bailey, the very beloved and revered Jack Russell terrier, and Jessica, the Boston terrier rescued from a trailer park in Florida—had both rounded the corner to older age. They no longer went on long walks with my dad through the woods (which we liked to call, in a nod to our one-sixteenth English heritage, The Wood), the main job description of my parents' dogs.

Uninterested in each other since they'd met seven years earlier when Jessica joined the family, the two spent a lot of time lying quietly under desks or splayed out on the cool terra-cotta tile in the kitchen. In the past year, Jessica had taken to retiring to my parents' bedroom immediately following her five P.M. dinner and not emerging again until my dad went upstairs to get her for the last pee of the night. Each night, he carried her down the stairs from the second floor like a football, just as he carried Bailey, who could no longer ascend, up them. With Jessica in hand, he would rouse Bailey as well and carry them both outside. He'd continue across the patio and onto that first patch of bleached-out brown grass where ideally the dogs should "go," as opposed to the patio or doormat (for which Jessica had recently developed a great fondness).

That wintry afternoon, as I sat with my mom in the den, we were reminiscing about the family dogs.

"Where did all the big dogs sleep when I was growing up?" I asked, remembering Max, our Irish wolfhound/English sheepdog mix, and Boswell, our tremendous (and tremendously sweet) English mastiff. "Were they all in your and Dad's room?"

"Yes, our room," Mom answered, nodding. "They all slept on the bed."

*Of course they did*, I thought. But I remembered my parents' bed from the house I grew up in, a very big four-poster, high off the ground, challenging to get up and into—at least from my then vantage point. Getting into that bed wouldn't have been a problem for Max, who in my memory (and I'm pretty sure in reality) could leap both tall buildings and the fence that led to the golf course our backyard abutted in a single bound. But it would have posed a problem for Boswell not only because of her thick, bull-like body, but also because of her fearfulness. Boswell, the biggest, fiercest-looking dog ever to live under our roof, was a dog for whom the ringing of the doorbell was like a death knell. One chime would send her running at warp speed, fur flying off her body, down the long hallway to the kitchen, where she would dive, any chairs in her way be damned, under the kitchen table and remain there, teeth actually chattering (we called it, fittingly, the "teeth chatter"), sometimes for hours.

"How did Boswell get onto the bed?" I asked.

"Oh," my mom said, "Bos was lithe." As she said this she leaned forward and made a rolling movement with her shoulders: my petite one-hundred-and-ten-pound mother approximating the motion with which our hundred-and-sixty-pound English mastiff would hoist herself bedward. My mom's eyes lit up as she did this, at the memory, at all of it.

Later that night, we were sitting again in the same room, the same chairs. My dad walked through the den, Jessica under one arm, Bailey sighing heavily at what was surely the annoyance of being hauled out into the cold for a pee, under the other. My ebullient, buoyant, still-young Carlie hopped along behind them very much like Sarah Jessica Parker's Sandi walking on the beach next to Steve Martin in *L.A. Story.*

"All right, ladies," I heard him say as the side door swung shut behind him and he escorted the three of them out to that first stretch of lawn. Through the glass doors of the den, I could see the older dogs ambling gingerly and, as soon as they could, turning back toward the house. I could see Carlie's white fluffy upright tail bouncing as she pranced around the farther reaches of the backyard no longer visited by Bailey and Jessica.

A question popped, unwanted, into my mind. Maybe it was an indelicate question, because of the obvious advancing age of their current crew, but in the way someone who's into therapy or yoga will espouse the many benefits of regular practice, in the way a dedicated attendee of spin classes will insist that if only you could get yourself to Soul Cycle, it will be the best forty-five minutes of your day, people who fall in love with a dog breed believe, with fervor, that others would really, truly benefit from opening up their lives and hearts to that same breed. I am an attendee of therapy and yoga and spinning. I can really see the benefits of the personal insight, mental clarity, and cardiovascular activity I get from all three (to say nothing of the leg-toning benefits of a regular spin routine). But unless specifically asked about my thoughts on these matters, I do not espouse. This is not so with my thoughts on Westies. Ever since I've had Carlie, whenever anyone has expressed an interest in getting a dog, I'll trip over myself to sing the praises of the breed.

So from the moment I got Carlie, I have been convinced

that my parents should get themselves a Westie. When the loss of their first Boston terrier ushered in the first time in the past forty years that they'd had only two dogs, this preoccupation kicked into an even higher gear. Occasionally, I'd inquire: "So you think you'll get a Westie?"

My dad, a key member of the Carlie Admiration Society, always and without hesitation said, "Yes." It was Mom who wavered.

"I don't want to hurt Carlie's feelings," she explained, "but I'd really like to get another Jack."

"Jane, don't you remember what it was like?" My father was referring to years one through thirteen of Bailey's life, in which she would bark shrilly for a good ten to fifteen minutes whenever anyone, even—especially—my parents, would walk in the front door. My mom would not hear him.

I'm a card-carrying member of the If You Don't Get the Answer You Like the First Time, Ask Again Club. I asked it that night.

"Do you think you'll get a Westie?" I asked that night in February. My mom looked off into the middle distance for a moment. Something in me knew before she answered. Of course, I knew that she wasn't going to say, "Yes, I'll get a Westie." But worse than that, far worse than that, I knew before she answered that she wasn't going to say what she usually said, the part about getting another Jack Russell terrier.

"You know," she said, "I just don't think I want any more dogs."

I stared back at her. *The horror.* To say that my parents without dogs are like cornflakes without milk lacks the necessary gravitas, it lacks the necessary everything. My parents without dogs goes against everything I've ever known. It goes against the natural order of the world. It's like life without . . . happiness, without . . . joy. It's like life without, well, life. Like giving up the good parts; it was to me like the death of hope.

"Mom," I said, "that's the craziest thing I've ever heard."

"It's very difficult," my mom began by way of explanation. "We're trapped right now. Bailey can't walk up the stairs; Jessica can't walk down. Bailey needs insulin every two hours. Jessica needs a hundred medications. They're peeing all over the house. If Dad and I want to go somewhere, I can't put them in a kennel in this state, at this stage of their lives. I can't go away, I can't leave them with someone else like this."

I nodded; I agreed with all of this. I don't like to think about it at all; I don't even like to touch keys on a keyboard that will type out words that have anything to do with Carlie's mortality. But be that as it may, in the sadly, horribly unavoidable event of the last twinkling moments of Carlie's twilight years, over my dead body would I leave her in a kennel. I would no sooner leave her locked in the kitchen even if she were peeing all over the house. I'd never go away on a trip knowing she might not be there when I got home. I understood, perfectly, everything my mom was saying. But

I couldn't, not even a little bit, wrap my head around what she said next.

"I've had a lot of dogs," she said. She paused; maybe it was a bit cinematically, or maybe that's just how I'm remembering it. Then she added, "I've had a lot of great dogs. I think I'm done. I think we're done."

Oh, dear God.

I didn't know what to do. I didn't know what to say. I wasn't sure there was anything I *could* do. I decided right then that now was not the time to push it. I knew the idea of getting a puppy while Bailey still inhabited this earthly coil was vehemently opposed.

"Think how she would feel, if there were a puppy here, someone who was more adorable than Bailey, someone who got more attention," my father had once explained.

"I would never do that to her," my mother had concurred.

I filed my thoughts of parental Westies away.

A few months later I was getting a manicure at the nail place right near my apartment. There was a woman in my direct line of vision, getting one of those ten-minute back massages, the kind where you sit in those special chairs, with bent knees and your face through a padded opening. It was warm out that day; it might even have been past Memorial Day if her sartorial selection was any indication: She wore gold ballet flats, white linen pants, and a bright green shirt. On her wrist a jumble of gold bracelets complemented her gold shoes. I couldn't see her face, submerged as it was in the padded part of the massage chair, but she had very thick light blond hair pulled back in a ponytail. There were sunglasses on top of her head. I liked her outfit. Particularly the shirt. Unusual for me: I don't really go in much for shirts. Yes, of course I wear them, but they're never the first item of clothing I'm drawn to in a store. I tend to go to dresses over pants and shirts, mostly for the reason that with a dress, the bulk of the outfit is done. I often feel confused by fashion and prefer to avoid weighty subjects like the combining of pants or skirts and shirts. My moments of fashion inspiration are few. That day at the nail place, I was inspired by the bright green shirt. I decided to embrace it. As I sat at the nail dryer and the woman in the bright green shirt stood up from her massage chair, I saw that her shirt wasn't some elusive find. The navy blue polo pony on her chest revealed the object of my sartorial desire to be your standard-issue short-sleeved knit polo shirt from Ralph Lauren.

Though I live only five blocks away from the Ralph Lauren flagship store on Madison Avenue, I didn't buy it there. I went home from my manicure, walked and fed my dog, and then went to RalphLauren.com and typed in "women's polo shirt." I briefly considered whether I wanted slim or traditional fit, debated the pros and cons, and ultimately went with traditional. I added the bright green—stem green to be exact—shirt to my virtual shopping basket.

A week or two went by and I didn't think about it. Another week went by, and I did. One afternoon it occurred to me that some time had passed, more time than the customary two to three days UPS takes to deliver goods ordered online. I wondered if I'd done something like stopped a screen too early, at the "review your order" page, and never completed my order, never even bought the shirt. This was a possibility. I've done similar, if not exact, things before. I went to RalphLauren.com to investigate.

At first, it didn't seem that there was any error. When I went to my recent order history, it said that the shirt had been shipped and delivered. It was no longer in transit, it had arrived safely at its destination. Though there is no doorman at my building to collect packages that are delivered, the packages for residents are all left, very charmingly I've always thought, on the mantel of the lobby fireplace.

Flummoxed, I picked up the phone to call customer service. This is what had happened: A few years ago, whenever I was getting a baby gift for friends, I'd get them an infant polo with their new baby's monogram on it. I would order these gifts from RalphLauren.com and have them wrapped and sent directly to the babies. RalphLauren.com dutifully kept a record of these addresses. So Andrew Ballard, age three, resident of the city of Baltimore and most recent recipient of an infant polo, had my bright green shirt.

Though I had not seen them recently, Andrew's parents are long-standing, dear friends. I grew up with Doug and have known his wife, Liz, since they started dating in college. In situations like these, I believe it's best to deal with the wife. I composed an e-mail or two before sending one that I thought included the appropriate but not overdone amount of sheepishness. I explained that I'd ordered a green shirt from Polo and sent it accidentally to Andrew. I added that because I really did *want* the shirt, I would be grateful, indebted really, if Liz would use the enclosed receipt to return the shirt to RalphLauren.com so that I could then order one that would be sent to me. I acknowledged that I knew this was a pain, apologized for inflicting a post office journey on a busy working mom of two, but greatly appreciated anything she could do.

A day or two passed, and Liz replied. *That's so funny*, she began. *Because you know how we moved two years ago?*

Yes, I thought, I actually did know that. I began to lose hope, but I read on. Liz wrote that the people who'd bought her and Doug's house had recently called to tell her of a package that was delivered for Andrew. Liz wrote next that she'd swing by the old house in the next week or so and mail the shirt back to me.

Back to me! Even better. *Thank you, Liz!* I wrote. *Thank you, thank you.* I included additional apologies for putting her out, and also thought to myself that of all the baby gifts I have sent out (I have sent out *a lot*), if I had to send a shirt I had intended for myself to any of them, I was lucky it was to Liz. Liz is the type of person who, if she had two weddings to attend in a weekend, would find a way to go to both. She'd go to a rehearsal dinner in Maryland and be at a reception in Vermont the next day. She worked things out, she did her best, she showed up for her friends. I was making plans to go to a wedding once in Maine and I asked a mutual friend if Doug and Liz were going to be there. I learned Doug would, and Liz had another event but was trying to figure it out.

"Liz will figure it out," I'd said.

"She will," the mutual friend had agreed. "If Liz has to rent a canoe and paddle up the eastern seaboard to the wedding, lit only by moonlight, she will."

I knew Liz would come through with the shirt.

A week later Liz e-mailed to say she was sorry she hadn't sent it yet, things had been crazy, but she'd get it done soon. I wrote back: *No problem, of course.* And then we e-mailed about the Fourth of July. Liz, Doug, and their kids would be going to Doug's parents' for the long weekend for a golf tournament that the group of guys I grew up with and am still friends with played in every summer. I wrote that I'd be there, too. I'd be out on Long Island for two weeks dog-sitting for Bailey and Jessica and finishing a book. A plan was made! Liz would come with the boys to visit while Doug was playing in the golf tournament. We'd go to the beach, all of us. Win-win! A long overdue catch-up with my friend *and* my green shirt.

On the eve of our plan, I e-mailed Liz to confirm. I was very happy to have a social break from a weeklong stretch of writerly seclusion. As Saturday came and I still hadn't heard anything back, I thought that, very fond of Liz though I was, I was fine if she didn't have time to come over, but now it was possible that the entire summer would go by and I'd never see the shirt.

As Saturday turned into Sunday, I sat at the shoreline using my hand as a makeshift visor over my eyes to shield them from the sun, all the better to see any oncoming canoes being paddled by Liz. None came.

A text from Liz arrived late Sunday. *Crazy busy weekend!* it began. There was a *Sorry we missed you*, followed by something I did not want to hear: She'd left the shirt with Doug's parents. I should just call Mrs. Ballard (Liz referred to her by her first name) to arrange a time to go over there and pick it up. She included the Ballards' phone number, though she didn't have to. I still know a select number of my childhood friends' phone numbers by heart.

*Aw, damn it all to hell*, I thought, *I really don't want to pick up the shirt from the Ballards.* I told myself I didn't want to pick up the shirt from the Ballards because I don't like the Ballards. That made sense. Or, it would make sense if it were even the littlest bit true. But the thing was, and the thing is, that I don't dislike the Ballards at all. I like the Ballards just fine. They are very nice people. What it was, what it is, is this: There are a lot of things I like about being single. I like independence and solitude. I get a jolt of happiness at the thought that most of the time I don't have to answer to anyone, in the knowledge that I can, within reason, do whatever

I please. I like the best-is-yet-to-come aspect of it, the thought, the hope, the sense that (elusive though he has thus far proved to be) my great love is still ahead of me.

In New York City, I have many single friends—friends who are successful, happy, and leading bright, shiny lives that do not include spouses. But on Long Island, where pretty much every one of the friends I grew up with met their spouses in college or a year or so after, I become The One Who Never Got Married. Shame wells up. It feels like finding a husband is a basic, fundamental thing that I have failed at. I feel it sharply around my childhood friends. I feel it tenfold around their parents.

*Why isn't she married? What went wrong there?* I believe that these are the questions that my childhood friends secretly think. It is my knowledge-from-experience that these are the very questions their parents not only think, but ask.

I have always loved the expression *take one for the team*. I like the way it sounds; I like the sense of sportsmanship and community and selflessness it brings to mind. I'll use it whenever I can, and sometimes even when technically I can't. I used it right then. I wondered if maybe, after all, the green shirt needed to take one for the team? Only there wasn't really a team. And if there was, I was the only one on it. *Yikes*, I thought. And though I am afraid of shame, I dialed the Ballards' number.

The next day, an uncharacteristically roasting one-hundred-degree day with all of the characteristic Long

Island humidity thrown in for good measure, I set off in my mother's station wagon for the Ballards', to retrieve, at last, my shirt.

"Aw, Alison! Alison!" Mrs. Ballard—a woman who has a first name but whom I can only ever think of as Mrs. Ballard—said as she answered the door. "What a story, what a story, but I'm not saying anything. I'm not saying *anything*. Liz said she had a shirt you ordered and I didn't even ask why."

Whether or not it's true, whether or not I'm a touch more paranoid than anyone has a right to be, I imagined that she *had* asked. Liz and Doug had told her, and then there was a Ballard family group eye roll and a chorus of *Oh, that Alison. Can't get it together to order a shirt correctly! No wonder she can't get herself a husband.*

"Yes, I was sorry I missed Liz," I said.

"Well, you know how it is when they come into town," Mrs. Ballard began. I nodded even though, actually, I didn't really know. I had not seen all that much of them recently. And when I had, it had been at events in New York City, or at weddings that had all happened years ago, but not so much on Long Island. "Doug played golf with Craig and Eric, and while they did Liz and Craig's wife and Eric's wife went to the beach club with all the kids."

Craig's wife: Samantha. Eric's wife: Jenna. I'd known them all for years; they, too, were my friends.

"Oh, yes, right," I said, as if, of course, I knew that. And for a long moment it was completely awful. And then, it was as if I'd always known exactly what was going to happen: My friends had become my married friends, and then they had become my married friends with kids, and then they had moved forward in their lives without me. I looked down, toward Mrs. Ballard's hands, to see if maybe the green shirt, perhaps still in its box, was right there with her, ready to be handed over and that would be it.

"Do you have a minute to come in?" Mrs. Ballard asked me. "Would you like an iced tea, or are you rushing off somewhere?"

"No, nowhere," I said, dazed. "Thank you, I'd love an iced tea."

I followed Mrs. Ballard into the kitchen. There, Mr. Ballard joined us. The pleasantries began, the *How are yous*, the *How are your parents*, the *Yes, of course I would love to see pictures of the grandchildren, seeing as how I missed them this weekend.* Throughout, I braced myself for the question, for the *And what about you, are you thinking about getting married?*

First, Mr. Ballard inquired, "What are you doing for work these days?"

"Oh," I replied, "I'm still writing. I'm a writer."

"What do you write?"

"I write novels," I told him. "And essays."

And then I waited for the *Why aren't you married?* question. But it didn't come. I wondered if, all these years into it, they'd given up on me. And suddenly right there, on a hundred-degree day, in the heavily air-conditioned refuge of the Ballards' kitchen, as I eyed my green shirt, still in its box, on the counter, I wondered if maybe the death of hope had nothing at all to do with my parents' lack of interest in future dogs.

I clutched the iced tea that Mrs. Ballard had given me and didn't say anything else, and neither, for a moment or two, did the Ballards. And then: a scratch at the door. It was then, so strangely only then, that I remembered the wonderful variety of dogs the Ballards had had while I was growing up. No family I knew growing up rivaled the menagerie that was my childhood home, but if there had been an award for a well-played distant second, it would go to the Ballards. Over the years they boasted golden retrievers, Bernese Mountain Dogs, Labradors.

At the sound of the scratch at the door, Mrs. Ballard's eyes lit up and so, too, did Mr. Ballard's. An energy, light and happy and expectant, filled the kitchen. Mrs. Ballard got up and opened the sliding glass door that led from the kitchen to the deck, a deck I can remember being built sometime around eleventh grade. In walked, I kid you not, a Jack Russell terrier puppy. By my guess, six, maybe seven, months old.

Mrs. Ballard bent down and picked up the puppy. He was little, perfectly adorable, and (unlike the nonstop barking machine I remember Bailey being from puppyhood clear through her first decade) remarkably mellow. It reminded me, vividly, of the moment that I first laid eyes on Spanky the Shar-Pei puppy in the entrance hall of the house I grew up in.

I watched as Mrs. Ballard brought the puppy all the way up to chest height, held him close, leaned in, and kissed him right there on the softest part of his neck. I thought first of Carlie, my own terrier, and then I thought of Bailey, at home, most likely snoozing in the corner of the kitchen that she liked best.

"Awwww," I said without even realizing I was about to say it, the universally accepted word for *Your dog is sooo cute.*

"This is Ranger," Mrs. Ballard told me proudly as Mr. Ballard looked on, smiling.

"Great name," I said, and almost involuntarily again, I held out my arms.

"Do you want to hold him?" Mrs. Ballard asked, and as I nodded eagerly, yes, I thought right then that it was the best question any parent of a high school friend had asked me in recent years.

"Absolutely," I said, and then, as soon as he sat happily in my lap, "Hi, Ranger."

"Your mom and dad have a Jack Russell terrier, right?" Mrs. Ballard asked me.

My mom and Mrs. Ballard had not been particularly friendly with each other for the nine years that Doug and I had been in school together. I think it's safe to say my mom and Mrs. Ballard have not laid eyes on each other since our high school graduation. I still have a picture of me and Doug and Craig on that day, in our red and black caps and gowns, all wearing sunglasses. But my mom and Mrs. Ballard do share a hairdresser: Guillaume. He comes to the house. He knows everything about everything, and shares it.

"Yes." I nodded. "Bailey."

"They've had her a long time," Mrs. Ballard said next, less a question than a statement, the passing on of information gleaned from a session with Guillaume.

"Yes. She's getting up there," I said, and then, not altogether cognizant that I was speaking out loud, "I'm not really sure what my mom is going to do."

Mrs. Ballard nodded and sighed. I think I did, too. I played with Ranger. Mrs. Ballard left the room. She returned a moment later with a business card and handed it to me.

"It's where I got Ranger," she explained. "A wonderful breeder, fantastic dogs."

I bounced Ranger on my lap and said to him in the voice that everyone reserves for adorable puppies, "I'm sure they are if they're anything like you."

"You give that to your mom," Mrs. Ballard directed me. "You know, when she's ready."

"Thank you, Mrs. Ballard," I said. "Really."

"Alison, Alison," she said. "All these years? How many years is it? You call me Brenda!"

I left the Ballards that day with my bright green polo

shirt and a business card for the breeder from whom Mrs. Ballard got Ranger. I left the Ballards with one of those elusive warm, fuzzy feelings. I'd had a really nice visit with the parents of one of my favorite friends from my childhood, a person who was part of a group that would always be important to me, always be so treasured, always be a big part of who I was, even if they were no longer a part of my day-to-day, or month-to-month, or even year-to-year life.

When my parents called to check in on the dogs, the house, me, I mentioned that I'd gone over to the Ballards' and that they had a Jack Russell terrier puppy.

"Very mellow," I said, hoping that part could be relayed to my dad at some necessary, crucial, strategic moment.

"Yes," my mom said. "Guillaume told me that Brenda Ballard had a new Jack puppy and that it was a really neat dog."

"He really was."

"Yes, Guillaume says that. Always says what a sweet puppy he is," Mom said, revealing Guillaume to be a likeminded comrade, but not revealing much more than that. I left it there. I hoped that there were ellipses at the end of the last thing my mom had said. I didn't say anything else on the matter, and neither did she.

In the piles of mail, bills, catalogs, and magazines I'd collected, separated, and sorted out for my parents while they were away, right on top I left the card for Ranger's breeder. In the unlikely event that this was not obvious enough, I included a Post-it: *from Brenda Ballard.*

I noticed on a subsequent visit home, as I was looking for a pen in my mom's desk—I was totally looking for a pen—that she had stashed the Jack Russell terrier card there.

A few weeks ago, my parents came into New York City to have dinner. Because my cousin Anthony has recently embraced veganism, and persuaded his mom (my mom's sister) to do so, too, my mom and I had developed a nascent interest in eating a more plant-based diet. Because of this, we were at Candle 79, a vegan restaurant in my neighborhood that serves a fantastic dish of spaghetti and wheat balls. We were seated by the window, looking out onto Seventy-ninth Street, our conversation peppered with observances of the canine passersby.

"Did you see that pair of bulldogs?" my mom asked.

"No, where?" I said, turning around.

"They're too far now, they just turned the corner. But how about this one coming this way?"

"Oh, that's a very good dog," my dad said. "Now, if a person is vegetarian and not vegan, they can have fish?"

"Yes."

"And cheese?"

"Yes," my mom told my dad. "But you know, if you'd like, you can get a grated soy cheese for your wheat balls." Then, outside on the dusky sidewalk—dusky because though we were at this point halfway through our dinner it was only about six thirty; my parents had to be home in time for Bailey's last insulin shot of the day—a pair of wire-haired Jack

Russell terriers walked by. They walked with an older gentleman, a man with good posture and an air of dignity, who wore a trench coat, scarf, and dapper hat, the kind of well-dressed and polished man that my own father is, the kind who seems so beyond the capabilities of the majority of men of my own generation. I, sitting across the table from my parents next to each other, nodded out the window and pointed so that my parents could see them, too.

I have joked that in the event that I ever have another person, I will get Carlie another dog. I have more morbidly joked that when Carlie hits twelve or thirteen years old, I will get a puppy because in the event of Carlie's big walk, I will need some serious backup.

Dogs are unique and special and extremely loving and greatly loved. In no way do I mean to imply that they can be replaced. What I do mean to imply is that losing a dog, even just the thought of losing a dog, is so truly awful that maybe the only thing that makes it bearable is to know that there will be dogs to love again.

They both turned around to catch the Jacks sauntering down the sidewalk. Even before they turned back around to face me, I knew they were both smiling.

Maybe it was an indelicate question. Maybe it was perfectly timed. I didn't turn more to my mom or to my dad. I faced them both head-on.

"So," I said, "speaking of Jacks, are you guys still in the same place?" They started to answer at once, and then my dad, noticing this first, held back a moment and let my mom speak.

"No," my mom said. "I think we have a new plan. I think we're going to wait six months."

"If we just want to go to Nantucket for four days, or drive to the North Fork for lunch on the spur of the moment, we'll be able to," Dad said.

"And then," Mom continued, "depending on how we feel, we're going to get two dogs."

"Two dogs?"

"Yes," my dad spoke up. "A Westie . . ."

Even though we were in the midst of dinner in a dimly lit elegant restaurant, I cheered.

"And a Jack," my mom added. "I think a nice wire-haired Jack."

I nodded, sagely, full of wisdom, like the guru I right then believed myself to be.

"I still have the card you gave me from Brenda Ballard's breeder," she added.

I nodded, beamed. "He was a very nice dog," I said. "Very relaxed, very peaceful."

"Guillaume," my mom said, as my dad nodded next to her in enthusiastic agreement, "*always* says the exact same thing."

# 16

. . . . . . . . .

## You Tell Your Dog First

When you meet him at a party, you do not think much of him one way or the other. But when he sends you an e-mail, months after you meet him, asking you to go out for a drink, you say yes.

He suggests you meet at the Campbell Apartment, a bar in Grand Central Station. You've always liked the Campbell Apartment. You take the subway to Grand Central Station and when you walk up the stairs, he's standing outside the entrance. He tells you it's closed for a private party. He's wearing a red North Face pullover over a shirt and tie and the pants to a suit. You wonder about his suit jacket. And while you have, in different situations, been fond of a North Face pullover, you think that you do not like his style. You

walk through a light sleet to the Algonquin Hotel, a suggestion he makes, one that you think is thoughtful, because
you're a writer. You open your mind to the possibility that
there are things you had not seen. Just as you step off the
sidewalk to cross over Vanderbilt Avenue, just as you're
thinking that, style aside, he actually is much more physically attractive than you initially gave him credit for—you
think he looks like a young Bobby Kennedy—he says something about his roommate. He is thirty-eight years old. You
do not love that he has a roommate. You think to yourself,
*Aaaand . . . scene.*

As you sit down in the lobby bar of the Algonquin Hotel,
he tells you how he spent the weekend leading up to your date
reading your novel. You think what you always think when a
man you're on a date with tells you he read one of your novels.
You think of the *Seinfeld* episode in which Jerry is dating a
cashier and she breaks up with him because she doesn't like
his act. Because she can't be with someone if she doesn't
respect what he does, and Jerry says, "But you're a cashier."
Not that he's a cashier. He went to Columbia Journalism
School. It's more that you worry that he won't like your act.

He tells you he really enjoyed your novel. You forget
about the roommate. And once he pulls it over his head and
puts it aside, the North Face pullover, you have a really nice
date, one of the nicest you can remember having in a while,
and you think that has something to do with more than the
fact that you haven't had a date in a while.

Two days later he sends you an e-mail: *Tuesday night was lovely. Want to do it again?*

*Lovely* is a word you use. You get this e-mail sitting at a wine bar on a date with someone else (yes, you hadn't been on a date for a while up to that point, but when it rains, it pours). He, the someone else, had at that moment gone to the men's room, so you had taken out your phone. When he comes back to the table, you take any notions of taking your neighbor Korbin's advice to "keep a lot of lines in the water, at the very least until the sixth date" and throw them out the window. You look across the table at the man who took you to the wine bar and know he doesn't stand a chance.

On your second date, he, the journalist, takes you to dinner in Tribeca in a restaurant that used to be a stable and afterward to a bar in the East Village that is across the street from the hot-pink building in which you had the protagonist in your last novel live. Never in your entire history of novel writing or dating—long histories, both!—has anyone ever taken you for a drink across the street from a place you have written about.

On your third date he takes you to the Metropolitan Museum of Art. On your fourth date, he gives you a Pavement CD and you ask him if he read your second novel, the one in which your protagonist wonders if she'll ever again meet a guy who will reach into his jacket pocket and pull out a mix tape, and no, he's not wearing a jacket, and no, this isn't a mix tape, *but still.* On your fifth date, he tells you,

"I don't have anywhere else to be. The only thing I want to do is be with you."

You bring him, almost immediately, home to meet your dog. Yes, that could be a euphemism, but also, you do bring him home to meet your dog. You have envisioned this moment. You've played it out in your mind. The moment in which Carlie meets him: whoever he may turn out to be. Right before you walk into your apartment with him, you envision the rainbows! hearts! flowers! you are sure you will see. In the moments before it's about to unfold before you, you imagine him bending down, scratching Carlie behind one ear and then the other, and saying in a soft voice, "Hey there." You picture Carlie laying her ears back on her head and giving her best double-time low tail wag as she approaches him. You see in your mind's eye, as good a place as any to see things, that split second in which Carlie looks into his eyes and he looks into hers and they know: This is the beginning of something good.

You walk into your apartment and he doesn't bend down. He looks down at Carlie from his full height. Carlie doesn't lay her ears back or low tail wag, not even a little bit. Carlie shows tooth and barks at him ferociously. Carlie turns and runs from the room.

"Oh," you say, as you try not to read too much into it. You succeed in not reading too much into it. Carlie has, after all, on one or two occasions, usually in the elevator, been a bit of a man-hater. You go into the kitchen and grab a treat from Carlie's treat canister and hand it to him. He looks at you blankly.

"You can give that to her," you suggest.

"Oh," he says, and takes the treat from you. He holds the treat out in front of him, like it's dirty. Carlie does not emerge from your bedroom to retrieve it. You think how at times Carlie has been indifferent to guests; sometimes she plays it close to the vest, but more often, she's much nicer than this. You think of the time recently when your friend Javi came over and Carlie sat on the couch between you, and as you and Javi talked she rested her head on his upper thigh and gazed up at him adoringly. Javi is a favorite friend and a wonderful, kind person. For this reason and many others, her inherent wisdom chief among them, you have always thought Carlie to be a great judge of character. You hope that Carlie is wrong about this one. You hope that Carlie is just off her game. It happens to everyone. It's happened enough to you.

In the weeks that follow, you feel certain that Carlie is wrong about him. In the weeks that follow, you consider once or twice that even though you have never been entirely sure what the question is, he could possibly be the answer.

"Having Carlie in your apartment is like having a little lamb in your apartment," he says to you one night. You find this adorable and tremendously endearing. You find him adorable and tremendously endearing. You're sure Carlie will warm up.

He calls you, late-ish one night, on your cell phone. You have just left dinner with a friend. As you walk up Fifth Street, you hear him take a deep breath. And then he asks you, "You know how I work with my ex-girlfriend?"

And you say, "No, I don't know how you work with your ex-girlfriend," because you don't; because in fact, on the subject of ex-girlfriends and for that matter ex-boyfriends, you can remember verbatim the conversation you had on this subject. It was late, you were falling asleep, and you'd inquired as to any ex-girlfriends and he said he'd broken up with someone months earlier but it wasn't a big deal. Had never been a big deal.

And then he'd said, "Do you hear that?"

And you'd said, "No, what?"

And he had said, "That's the sound of me not asking you about your ex-boyfriends because it doesn't matter; the only thing that matters is right now." And it hadn't seemed even one one-hundredth as cheesy when he spoke it as it does right now.

"Well, yeah," he says through his cell phone. "I work with my ex-girlfriend." And as it turns out, things aren't quite over with the ex-girlfriend, and he's not really sure where that leaves the two of you but he . . . can't. He says that—"I can't"—a few times more, and shortly you get off the phone and hail a cab. You go home and tell your dog. You cry.

You pine a little bit. You and your friend Robin compare him to dating Brigadoon, and you wonder if people missed

Brigadoon a lot when it was gone, even though they hadn't known it for very long at all. Robin also tells you that the way these things go, it's not like it's really going to work out with the ex-girlfriend, because that never works, and he'll be back, he'll call you again and want to come back, but by the time that happens, you won't want him.

"Right," you say to Robin, "I won't want him, not even a little bit." You say this even though you don't mean it.

A few months later, he calls. It didn't work out with the ex-girlfriend. And though there is now a large part of you that thinks this guy is no good, this guy is not a stand-up guy, this guy broke up with you on the phone, there isn't anyone else you like. Also, you're at the point in your novel writing where you haven't really been getting out much to meet new people. You know that these are not the best reasons to take someone back, to be with someone in the first place. But yet.

Things start up again. Very quickly. You think it's good he came back, and it's better that you let him. You tell your dog first. You tell her you're happy. You talk to her dreamily of second chances and you tell her you really like him. She stares at you blankly. One morning as he is walking past her, Carlie bites at his pant leg, only he's not wearing pants. You notice, much to your chagrin, that he has fallen down on the job when it comes to toenail clipping.

"Why didn't you get a beagle?" he asks you one evening.

"I don't understand the question" is your answer. You

begin to consider that he sometimes acts like an idiot when he drinks.

Shortly, whenever he walks into your apartment, Carlie moves into the other room. Privately, you ask her to make more of an effort. It is not immediately following this request but soon enough after it that you are sure your dog is a genius: One night, as he is reclining on your couch, she jumps up next to him and rests her chin on his ankle.

He turns toward you. "Is it okay if she doesn't sit up on the couch with me?" he asks. You start at this point to not be able to ignore it.

He's not mean to Carlie. Mean to Carlie you could never abide. But he's not nice to her. Once, he came over and right when he did you had to run to the deli to get something. You left him in your apartment with Carlie and when you came back Carlie was right by the front door and he was on the couch engrossed in the paper.

"Was Carlie sitting right by the door the whole time I was gone?" you inquired.

"I have no idea what she was doing," he said. Carlie looked up at you with an expression you had trouble reading, and you looked away from Carlie and across the room to see the journalist folding his newspaper lengthwise and creasing the edge and then setting it on your coffee table and then looking up at you and smiling in a way that you also found yourself unable to read.

You start to have a lot of trouble with the novel you're

# You Tell Your Dog First

writing. This is nothing so new; you have a lot of trouble writing every novel you've ever written. One night you tearfully tell the journalist that you're having a really bad time, that you're just not sure the story is working the way you want it to. You think at the time that you're talking just about the book you're writing, even though it would be obvious to anyone else that you're talking about more than that. You think that since he's a writer, too, he'll get it. He does not, however, get it. At this tearful confession of the trouble you're having, he does not offer anything that could be called deep or even casual understanding. He sort of just tilts his head and looks at you as if he thinks you're crazy.

"I'm just feeling kind of overwrought," you say. "It's just that I've been writing all day, for days."

"I write all day, every day," he tells you. "Why is this such a big deal?"

It is not just that, you know it's not just that, but you start, after that, to think in a few relationship-speak clichés. The sentence *I'm not sure he's on my side* begins, with some frequency, to pop into your head. You wonder if maybe Carlie dislikes him so much because she knows something you don't. Or knows something you do, but when it comes to wanting to know it, you don't. Maybe she knows that he has darkness in his heart. Or worse yet, also more likely, maybe Carlie knows that on the subject of you, he doesn't have anything in his heart. You find yourself hoping more than anything else that if it doesn't work out, it won't really

191

hurt. But you know that it will because these things, when they end, do tend to hurt. Instead you hope it won't be the thing that makes you want to give up. You hope it'll turn out to be nothing.

One night he suggests going to dinner in Brooklyn. He knows a great place. You're not really in the mood to go all the way to Brooklyn. You're in the subway and you're sitting with him on a bench on the platform for the 4/5 train at Fifty-ninth Street. You don't know what's going to happen. From somewhere—you think it might be coming from across the tracks—you hear a beeping. He turns to you and says, "What's that beeping?"

You turn to him and look at him and think that, still, he has really pretty blue eyes. You consider saying to him, *This whole time I've been a robot, and the beeping means that now I'm going to explode.* You consider saying to him, *I'm hoping it's nothing.* Instead you look back at him and say, "I don't know."

You continue to flip out a little bit over your novel. You are helpless in the face of trying not to flip out a little bit over your novel. You know this. You know this is what always happens; you just don't want it to happen now. You think of the Algonquin Hotel, the visit to the building in which your protagonist lived, of how when you first started dating, the thing he liked most about you was that you wrote novels. You realize you are still thinking in clichés, or maybe that's platitudes, but the things that he liked so much about you

are becoming, you're pretty sure of it, up there on a list of
the things that annoy him. You suspect he is definitely not
the one. You suspect, but are not quite ready to admit, that
your dog was right all along.

It will end several weeks later when you are visiting your
sister in Los Angeles, and he forgets your birthday. You call
him the day after your birthday to ask him if he forgot your
birthday which is, in and of itself, a stupid thing to do,
because: He forgot your birthday. He will tell you that
yes, he forgot and then he will not apologize but he will say,
"Happy Birthday." You will say it no longer counts.

He will tell you that it is time to face facts, and that you
and he are not meant to be. He will tell you, on the phone,
as you sit in a hotel room in West Hollywood, the day after
your birthday, which he forgot, that life is hard and dating
you makes it harder. He will say that even though you and
he were awful together, there was a lot of it that was fun.

He will ask you, "Wasn't there a lot of it that was fun?"
You will be unsure whether he is trying to make you feel
better, or make himself feel better, and for both, or neither,
of those reasons, you will not answer him.

You fly home to New York the next day. At LAX, you go
immediately to the airport bookstore. For the first time ever
you blow right past fiction and head straight for self-help.
You buy a book called *It's Called a Breakup Because It's Broken* because you think it could help.

As you board the plane, you want to try to find some sort

of inner Zen. You try to think of an interview you listened to recently on NPR with a yogi, and how the yogi said that even the people who harm you and hurt you are your teachers. Mostly, though, you drink white wine on the plane and lean against the window so that the tattoo-covered surfer next to you can't see you trying not to cry. Suddenly, the *he's not on my side* thoughts don't seem so cliché. Because right then, right there, as you sit on a plane, trying not to cry, clutching a glass of white wine in one hand and a copy of *It's Called a Breakup Because It's Broken* in the other, you are a really bad cliché.

Sooner, much sooner rather than later, you go about the business of pulling yourself together, of picking up the pieces, of dusting yourself off. You remind yourself that you're good at this. You remind yourself that you have not, ever, considered that in these situations there was anything else to do. You tell your friends that he was a terrible person. Because they are your friends, all of them agree. More than two say they thought so all along. Your friend Robin will tell you that if you'd written this whole thing out as a book proposal, an editor would have told you that it didn't make sense, that there was no motivation for the you character to want to be with the journalist character, that at every turn it was confounding. You will nod.

One night soon, you are at home watching a movie with your dog. The actor Jonah Hill is onscreen. You look at Jonah Hill and you are reminded of the journalist. You are, right then, able to see a somewhat uncanny resemblance between Jonah Hill and the journalist. Especially around the eyes. You turn to your dog, who is next to you, and you tell her what you should have told her a long time ago.

"You were right all along."

She looks back at you with her beautiful, liquidy, jet-black eyes and you are certain that as she does, she does not gloat. It is not her way. You believe that if she could talk, she would say to you, *I wish I'd been wrong.*

Before you've really forgotten, before you really let go, before you let the chips fall where they may, you think about going back in time, just for a minute. You want to go back to the night you sat with him on a bench inside the subway, waiting for a train. You want there to be a beeping. You want him to turn to you and say, "What's that beeping?" And you want to rewrite it; you want to turn back to him and say, "It means time's up."

# 17

## You Are Here

Whenever I visit a new place, I am struck almost immediately by the thought that I could live there. The actual location is not all that important. Granted, the nicer the place, the longer the feeling lasts, but the initial impulse can pop up almost anywhere. It could be Paris, Miami, the waterfront town in Connecticut to which a friend recently moved, a fly-fishing lodge in Idaho, or the apartment complex that is adjacent to the shopping center in Weehawken, New Jersey, where I meet my friend Wendy because we have determined it to be more or less equidistant between my apartment in New York City and her house, farther away in New Jersey.

When I travel, as soon as I'm at my destination, I immediately start to plan my future life there. I wonder about what type of home I'd have, where I'd walk my dog, and the people I'd meet. If I walk past a coffee shop, I'll speculate as to whether the coffee shops here in my new Paris/Miami/Connecticut/Idaho/New Jersey (fill in any other destinations you might like at will; I do) life will be ones in which I will write. I imagine what my friends will be like in this new place. Will I like them better or less than I like the people in New York? Will I be easily bored, homesick, or lonely? Will I pick up different hobbies, different hopes, dreams, fears?

I remain in this state of mind for anywhere from one to three days. I do not think that this *I could live here* quality is necessarily a desire to leave New York. I stay in Manhattan not out of necessity but out of want. I'm here by choice.

I've also always been of the mind that trips that take the traveler a bit out of her comfort zone can be the best kind. One summer I started thinking about just that. I started thinking about getting far away.

As soon as that thought crystallized, I remembered, years earlier, meeting the wife of a friend of a friend from Italy. She was an avid amateur archaeologist and went every summer to a small island off the coast of Sicily to work on a dig site. Her name was Elena, and she had told me that I was welcome to come along on a dig anytime. I had penciled it on my life list. I've never wished I were Indiana Jones (my fantasy alternative careers include but are not limited to marine biologist, Broadway actress, and dermatologist), but from the first time I'd heard about people taking trips to unearth ruins and discover artifacts from civilizations of the distant past, I thought I'd really like to do that, too. I started making phone calls. I asked my contact if his Italian friend's wife still went on that dig every summer.

Elena still went on a dig every summer, with a group of Italian archaeologists. It was run through the University of Bologna, and the island, I learned, was called Pantelleria.

I Googled Pantelleria. It was an island in the strait of Sicily in the Mediterranean Sea. It was sixty-two miles southwest of Sicily and just forty-three miles from the Tunisian coast. I discovered that archaeologists on the island had unearthed dwellings and artifacts dating to thirty-five thousand years ago.

I kept clicking. I clicked on every link I could find on the subject of Pantelleria. I saw a lot of maps. One map I remember more than the others: There was the vast expanse of Tunisia on one side, the boot of Sicily on the other. Almost perfectly in the middle, a tiny dot. This dot was labeled *Pantelleria*, with a little white arrow pointing to it; a white sign attached to the arrow said, *You Are Here*.

I stared at the dot, at the words *You Are Here*, and thought again, *I could be there.*

I sent e-mails to Elena in Italian, crafted with the Alta-Vista translator, expressing my desire to join the dig that summer. I now know that the AltaVista translator can do some extremely funky things to language. Elena wrote back to me to say that there was indeed room for another person.

We flew past formalities and moved on to flight plans and arrival dates.

I learned that it is not easy to get oneself from New York City to Pantelleria, but that any problem that can be solved by a two-day stopover in Rome is not such a problem. Then I enrolled in a six-week beginner Italian class. I spent three hours every Wednesday morning at a school that occupied an entire charming brownstone called Parliamo Italiano (which translates, rather optimistically, I thought, to "we speak Italian") trying to master basic conversational Italian with a couple from Brooklyn who were renting a house in Tuscany for the summer, a retired police officer, an aspiring chef, an heiress, and two ladies-who-lunch from Greenwich, Connecticut.

And soon enough, armed with new but yet sufficiently broken-in hiking boots, a selection of loose-fitting clothing, a wide-brimmed hat, and enough SPF 75 sunscreen (I burn easily) to slather a large horse from head to hoof, I departed for Pantelleria by way of Palermo and the aforementioned two days in Rome.

As my alarmingly small, propeller-style plane arrived in Pantelleria, I was concerned about whether I would recognize Elena, someone I had met only once, years ago, or be left wandering aimlessly, looking for her throughout the airport. As I deplaned and walked across the tarmac, I noticed that the airport was just one square room and my concerns over not being able to locate Elena began to dissipate. Those same concerns evaporated completely when I saw a group of five people, all wearing white T-shirts emblazoned in red with Italian words, one of which I definitely recognized: *archeologia*. I was instantly touched that the entire group had come to the airport to get me.

"Al-eee-sohn?" Elena said to me.

Her voice was lilting, lyrical, heavily accented. I loved the way my name sounded in an Italian accent.

"Al-eee-sohn?" she said again, because I had not answered, focused as I was on the niceness of her accent.

"I'm here!" I answered. I was there and very happy.

And then the five assembled amateur archaeologists—two men, three women—began speaking to me at once. I had no idea what they were saying. I looked back at them, wondering if it was possible to convey through nodding that I appreciated that they had all come to pick me up, and that though I wasn't all that proficient at Italian, I was looking forward to the dig. I wished I knew the words for *I've always wanted to do this*.

Even when they slowed down and spoke very slowly, even when they spoke one at a time and repeated themselves, at length, I still had not the slightest idea what they were saying. I rued all those times at Parliamo Italiano when I had been reluctant to try out my *frasi* in front of the group. I cursed those moments when I had completely spaced out, and those moments that usually occurred sometime around hour three when I had become much more interested in taking a look-see at my BlackBerry than I had been in practicing an inquiry as to where the post office was located.

"*Scusi?*" I said, politely, because I could no longer remember if that was the polite way of saying *Excuse me* or more of a slang way of saying it. Interspersed in the deluge of Italian words, I heard the English words *no matter* (a phrase it would turn out the Italians had fully embraced, along with a heavily elongated *o-kaay*) and also, I was almost sure of it, I'd heard the word *gelato*.

We left the small airport with my suddenly gigantic-seeming bag. It is said that one of the things people can learn when traveling is that they don't need nearly as much as they think they do. I, without fail, always forget this upon my return home. Our group of six dispersed into two groups of three, into two little cars that looked like miniature, low-to-the-ground Jeeps. I can no longer remember what they were called—I want to say they were named after an animal, something slow, perhaps industrious, a beaver, or maybe a muskrat.

We drove, one car after the other, down a twisting road, into the small, waterfront town that had stone buildings (each painted a different pastel color), walkways by the water (complete with cafés and shops), and a port full of sailboats. We did indeed get a gelato. I ate a zabaglione-flavored gelato while sitting on a ledge near the water along with the five Italians with whom I would be living for the next two weeks. I envisioned the very Indiana Jones attire that everyone would wear (I myself had acquired a special hat just for this trip). I pictured the dig site, imagined a large canopy setup, underneath which would be tables with maps and instructions, perhaps computer equipment and cold beverages for breaks. I listened to my new archaeological compatriots speaking in a language I thought I understood when it had been spoken very, very slowly to me in a classroom. The gelato was outstanding; the scenery—mountains of gleaming black volcanic rock looming over the colorful port—was picturesque and breathtaking. I was, after many days of traveling, after many months of planning, on a tiny island right in the middle of Sicily and Africa. I observed my group, sized them up, sussed them out. There was Elena and a couple her age, Giuseppe and Daniella, all of whom I am guessing were in their early sixties. There was Davide, who would turn out to be the foremost English speaker and thus chief communicator of the group, who seemed to be in his late forties, and his longtime girlfriend, Sonia, in her late twenties. Davide and Sonia were in fact real, professional archaeologists and traveled around the world on assignment. They would not be heading to the *università*-run excavation site that the rest of us would be reporting to each day. (At the thought of the excavation site, how I imagined the digging, the brushing of delicate and centuries-old rocks off with a precise tool, one that had a brush on it of course, and feeling completely immersed, and scholarly, and a part of a great and vast history all at once!) Rather, Davide and Sonia had come to the island simply because it was beautiful and a vacation spot, and their plan was to enjoy it as tourists rather than archaeologists.

I inquired slowly, directing my question to Davide, what he and Sonia would be doing in lieu of digging. He explained to me that they would have "holiday." They would go to the sea. They would see the island.

Immediately after that, I learned that due to a "mix-up"—another English phrase the Italians liked—at the university in Bologna, the archaeological van, all of the archaeological equipment, and for that matter, all of the other archaeologists had been delayed. Davide, Elena, Giuseppe, Daniella, e Sonia were "not certain" when the van would arrive, but until then, we, too, would have "holiday."

I felt a strong sense of initial disappointment at this news of dig delay. This disappointment was compounded by a longer-lasting sense of deep awkwardness at the fact that I was now, for all intents and purposes, on a beach vacation with five random Italian people.

We returned to our two cars and drove, one car after the other, up and down winding roads through hills of black rocks, vistas of sparkling Mediterranean water. We arrived at our house that was not technically a house but a *damusso*. On the island of Pantelleria the houses are all *damussi*, domed stone buildings designed to best withstand the heat. Dotted over the hillsides, mostly surrounded with stone fences, they looked like igloos, only designed for the sun.

As we entered the *damusso*, the clock on the kitchen wall said four fifteen. I was surprised to realize I'd been en route to the *damusso* for almost twenty-four hours. For the six of us, the *damusso* had two bedrooms and one bathroom. Giuseppe and Daniella had the master bedroom, I bunked with Elena in a small den in the back, and Davide and Sonia camped in a nook in the dining room.

I realized slowly that for the entirety of the trip, we would do everything as a group. Think of this scenario taking place in the United States: six unrelated and unknown-to-each-other Americans put together in a very small house for two weeks. It is the stuff that nightmares and reality television shows are made of. But in Pantelleria, it was not that at all. Everyone got along; everyone read books; everyone was energetic yet calm, and patient, and considerate of others. Granted, I could not understand a great deal of what was said, but I am nonetheless quite certain that was the case.

Elena was serene and knowledgeable and fully in love with everything about the island. After twenty summers spent on it, she still looked at everything with wonder. Daniella always inquired if it was too hot for me, if I had my sunscreen. One evening, we went over, word by word, a lecture she was preparing on Nathaniel Hawthorne for a seminar she taught. I loved her description of him: *E altero ha un solo desiderio: trovare l'amore.* He had only one desire: to find love. Giuseppe, a retired engineer, was our unofficial leader, and each night over dessert, which was usually *passito*, a wine made from special Pantesco (read Pantellerian) grapes, he would detail the next day's plans in a portion of the evening he called *La Programma*. Davide was the joker, always making everyone laugh. Sonia was young and vibrant and athletic. She took me hiking and snorkeling, and more than anyone I have met before or since, she could talk a blue streak. With the most excellent hand gestures.

They all had the ability to sit quietly and look at the scenery without the need for distraction. They stopped to look at the water, the rocks, the gardens. They noticed things. They read books every afternoon. No one toted around power bars, or water bottles, or venti coffee cups, or iPods, or cell phones when they walked. There was no "stuff." They excelled at just being.

Every day we would rise at seven, eat Nutella, and depart for one of several rocky beaches to spend the morning. We would bring with us a cooler containing six cups and one carton of ACE (pronounced "ah-chay"), an orange, lemon, and carrot (*arancia, limone, carota*) juice blend rich in vitamins A, C, and E. It was tasty and refreshing, and I wish they packaged it here. We would sit for hours on our mats on the rocks. I would perhaps a bit obsessive-compulsively slather myself in my SPF 75 sunscreen, and I think maybe the luxuriously olive-hued and tan-ready Italians would talk about that. There were no games, no lounge chairs, no chatter. There were the rocks, and the sea, and that moment. Until someone would stand up and declare, "Ah-chay!" and then we all would get up joyously and clap our hands and have a glass of orange juice.

By noon every day, the sun would have become so scorching, the temperature would have ratcheted up to about 112 degrees Fahrenheit, and we'd then leave the rocks. We would stop in town for a quick, light lunch (*pranzo*) or to pick up something to eat at the *damusso*. I do not know about all Italians, but these Italians, whom I quickly began to think of as *my* Italians, and as my friends, did not eat very much at all. Olives, tomatoes, bread in small servings, *Parmigiano* cheese, and tuna fish in olive oil made up most of our meals. In Pantelleria, in addition to being hotter than I think I have ever been in my life, I was a bit famished as well. After lunch, with the hot Pantesco sun still high in the sky, we would have three to four hours at the *damusso* because to venture anywhere else in the heat would be, as the Italians explained to me, "not safe." The Italians would read, talk under the canopy, or nap. Completely unaccustomed to the staggering heat, every day, immediately following *pranzo*, I headed to my room and promptly passed out.

Around four, four thirty, as the sun would be not quite descending, the group would prepare for an afternoon excursion. To signal the end of my siesta, Elena would call to me from her perch underneath the canopy.

"Al-eee-sohn," she would call. "Al-eee-sohn, where are you?"

"I am here," I would say as I emerged from my room. I always carried with me one hiking boot and one flip-flop. Elena would point to whichever footwear choice best suited the afternoon's excursion.

We hiked, visited ruins, drove cross-island to a farm to

buy Pantesco *capperi* (capers, plentiful in Pantelleria, and one of my favorite Italian words) and tomatoes. We shopped in town and swam in secret coves. I learned to wear my bathing suit even with hiking boots, as the opportunities to swim never ran out. One day, we spontaneously pulled to the side of the road and picked capers for hours. We scouted out ancient sarcophagi hidden in the hills; we partook of natural mud baths. By nine or ten each night, we'd be back under the canopy for a dinner that lasted for hours, plentiful on stories that I was slowly able to understand.

I practiced my Italian. Daniella and Elena, who had learned much of their English by way of reading children's books, bought me a copy of *Cenerentola* (Cinderella). I learned a lot from listening. I was partial to the phrases *Io ti aiuteró* ("I will help you") and *lieto fine* ("happy ending"). I had my favorite words: *snocciolato* ("without pits"), *capperi* (the aforementioned capers), *cagnolina* ("little dog"), and *randagio* (a wild dog of Pantelleria). I liked *cagnolina* because it reminded me of my own dog, whom I missed at home. I liked *randagio* in a different sort of way. I can remember well the scenery, the taste of the gelato, the overwhelming feeling of exhaustion from the heat, and just as well I remember the *randagi*, the way they skipped gracefully up the hills, a rust-red one I always looked out for who'd hang by the water on the route home from the town, the way he'd look out at the passing cars.

We spent long evenings under the canopy at our *damusso*.

The air would cool down a little, and by the end of the trip I'd picked up enough to tell the table, in grammatically correct Italian, what we'd done that day, and what we'd do the next day. To everyone's delight, mine absolutely included, all the Italians' English greatly improved. I learned to say *va bene* really well. It means "okay" or "it's fine." Of all the phrases I learned and practiced while in Pantelleria, *va bene* was both the one I said the most, and the one that I had needed to learn how to say. I was not always a person who said *va bene*. In Pantelleria, I was. As the days passed too quickly, as we sang Italian songs around the big table, I loved the island. I loved these people more.

Three days before I was scheduled to return to New York, the archaeological truck, complete with all the archaeological equipment and all the archaeologists, arrived.

Whenever I think of Pantelleria now, it is firmly divided into two parts: the before part and the digging part.

There was no canopy at the dig site, but it was set on a high cliff overlooking the clear sea, just far enough away that one could not get into it. The digging part was all at once fascinating, interesting, exhausting, and hard. I loved that there was the promise of coming across pottery that dated back to the eighteenth century B.C. I loved that after a day of excavation, the outlines of a wall from a twelfth-century village were visible. I did not love the fact that because of my newly discovered low tolerance for extreme heat and sun, I spent most of the time at the excavation site feeling as if I might pass out. Squatting for six hours in the blazing sun with a pickax and a selection of shovels while a bikini-clad Italian graduate student scolded me—"You're doing it wrong" and "No, not like that"—was not quite the Indiana Jones fantasy I had cracked it up to be.

Maybe it was because it was so hot there that I was not, as much as I loved being in Pantelleria, inclined to plan my life there. I didn't want to live there, but as my time there drew to a close, I didn't want to leave. I wanted to stay a bit longer, to hear my name called from the terrace a few more times.

*Al-eee-sohn*, I wanted to hear for a few more days.

*Al-eee-sohn. Where are you?*

*I am here*, I wanted to say.

On my last afternoon in the *damusso*, as I stopped into the kitchen for a quick glass of ACE, I noticed that the clock on the wall said four fifteen. It was only the second time in over two weeks that I'd looked at it. I thought of what a coincidence it was that it was the exact time I'd looked at it last and then felt remorse that it was somehow already so late in my last day on the island. A quick trip back to the kitchen about ten minutes later for the very purpose of looking at the clock a third time revealed that it still said four fifteen. It had been stopped on four fifteen the entire time I was in Pantelleria.

A few moments later, Elena wanted to be sure what time my plane took off. I took my ticket out of my bag to check.

"*Quattro e quindici*," I told her. Four fifteen. Really.

Later that afternoon, all six of us drove to the airport, in our two different cars. All six of us took my bag into the tiny Pantelleria airport and headed to the one check-in counter. Six of us double-checked that my bag would go from Pantelleria to Palermo and then on to Rome. Everything was checked, everything was ready.

As we'd sat around the table the night before, the Italians had given me a T-shirt that said *capperi* on it, because it was one of my favorite words, and they'd asked me to join them at the dig the next summer. I thanked them very much for asking and told them I would try, even though I knew that the experience I'd just had could never be replicated.

As I said good-bye to my five Italian friends and prepared to begin my two-day journey back to New York, Elena said to me, "We will wait for you in Italy."

Daniella added, "We will wait for you in Italy."

"We will wait for you in Italy," echoed Giuseppe, Davide, and Sonia.

My emotions exist on a plane that is quite close to the surface. I'm an easy cry under the seemingly least emotional of circumstances. That afternoon, I sobbed in the Pantelleria airport. I tear up a bit thinking about it even now. I hugged them all again, kissed them each on both cheeks again, said *arrivederci* and *mille grazie* and hurried through the gate. And though I cried the entire way through it, it was in its way a *lieto fine*, a happy ending.

I knew this before, I think I've known this all along, but

what I was reminded of right then was that at the end of every trip, no matter how long or how short, no matter how diligently I have planned my life there or not, no matter if I've loved it or hated it, one thing is always the same. I'm always ready, at the end, to come back to New York. I'm always ready to come home.

I love New York. And sometimes I hate New York. I have toyed at various times with leaving it. But I have always stayed.

Sometimes when I'm having one of those days, one of those days when nothing is going quite right, and usually it's raining, sometimes what I want most is to leave. But then, right as I'm contemplating a life in, say, Barcelona or Denver, I remember that I'm actually happy to be here.

It happens this way: I stop for a second, I close my eyes, I listen. I imagine I hear a lilting voice, speaking with an Italian accent.

*Al-eee-sohn. Where are you?*

I take a deep breath. I think about all the good things. I think about my family, my friends, all the cherished people in my life. I think about the fact that I actually get to be a writer. I think about my dog.

*Al-eee-sohn.* I hear it again. *Where are you?*

I open my eyes. Sometimes I even say it out loud:

*I'm here.*

# 18

· · · · · · · ·

# Fabio

"Have you met anyone?"

This is a question people ask of the single. This is a question people asked me a lot. I will ask it, or some variation of it, of my single friends.

"Have you met anyone?" "Are you seeing anyone new/special/interesting?" Not everyone likes this question. I remember once I ran into a friend—more a friend of a friend really, someone like a rung, maybe two, higher on the ladder above acquaintance. I ran into this woman at Barnes and Noble, the old one on Eighty-sixth Street that isn't there anymore. It was around the holidays and I was there buying presents when I saw her walking down the cookbook aisle toward me.

"Hi, Beth!" I called out.

"Hi, Alison!" she called back.

We talked for a while, got the *How are you*s out and the *What's new with you*s covered, and then I asked it: "Are you seeing anyone?" It was a question asked in passing, casually, really no big deal at all. Swear.

"You know," she snapped back at me, "I really hate that question."

"Uh-huh?" I think I said.

"It's like," she continued, "if I were seeing anyone, I would have told you. You would have known."

"Uh-huh." I nodded.

"I mean, it's fine," she continued. "It's just everyone asks me that all the time."

"I see," I said. I generally don't see it that way. With, yes, an exception or two, I usually look at that question as a cheering from the sidelines, a universal code for *we're all rooting for you*. An understanding that the person asking it and me, we are like-minded, we believe that everything will turn out well in the end. And it wasn't as if I'd had any less experience with the question than Beth did. Everyone asked me that question all the time. Not only did others ask, they predicted, oftentimes, various potential timetables.

"When your first book comes out," a friend told me, "you're going to become very famous and the press guy who takes you around from the *Today Show* to *Oprah* will become your boyfriend." A prediction that was at once charmingly optimistic and specific, and also obviously made by someone who didn't work in publishing. Nine out of ten book publicists are lovely young women and not potential dates. And nobody gets on *Today* or *Oprah* either.

As I prepared to depart for three weeks on the tiny Sicilian island where I'd be taking part in an archaeological dig, almost every person I spoke to about my plans said, "I'll bet you'll meet a guy there. An Indiana Jones type." Though I did wonder why, how, upon hearing of weeks spent on an island working on an archaeological dig, people's takeaway could be, *Alison can finally meet someone*, it didn't annoy me. I saw it (mostly saw it) as a collective cheering-on.

The same thing happened when I first got a dog.

"You're going to meet someone through your dog!" rallied the collective cry. I wondered then if maybe the collective everyone was getting impatient with my search.

"Ashleigh Banfield from CNN met her husband walking her dog in Central Park," a friend informed me. I actually knew that; I'd been a fan of Ashleigh Banfield's, and of her glasses. "And Ashleigh Banfield was well *into her thirties* when she met her husband," this friend added.

"Have you met any men, all that time walking your dog in Central Park?"

"Have you gone on any dates with anyone you met walking your dog?"

"Have you met *any* guys?"

"I haven't," I relayed. This type of conversation happened

anytime I mentioned how much I enjoyed the early-morning walks I took with Carlie when she ran off-leash and the park was filled with scores of dogs running free, how that hour was so full of joy, how it was my favorite part of every day.

I became worried at this point, less about the fact that I might never meet anyone, and more about the fact that I was, at the heart of it, letting all these people, all these friends, who had all the long, long while been rooting for me, down.

"No one?"

"No cute guys with dogs?"

"What about not-cute guys without dogs?"

"No," I gulped. "But it's not that I haven't met any *people*. I just haven't met any men. I've met a lot of crazy women."

That is my truth. I'm not trying to say something unkind about the women in New York. I love the women in New York. All but one of my closest friends, all my colleagues, and countless people I admire are women in New York. Just, my experience during off-leash hours in Central Park (in the early days of walking Carlie there) was that there were not any men to be met, and the women struck me as kind of crazy. For all I know they thought the same thing of me, and that's really okay.

As my years taking my dog to Central Park increased, I became more discerning about with whom I would walk. Eventually, I met Nancy, the woman who had Ian, Carlie's half brother, and a few other people I enjoyed spending time with: Lindsay, who lived next door to me and walked her

Shar-Pei, and Ellen, who had the gutsiest King Charles Cavalier spaniel I've ever known. I like them and view them as friends. I look forward to seeing them, but it was not always this way.

Maybe everything, including off-leash hours in Central Park, is just a continuation of high school. And you know how in high school the craziest, most friendless and annoying people would pounce on the newest students and claim them before said new students had a moment to gather their wits about them and run in the other direction? That's how it was in my high school, and that's how it was for me in Central Park. I was befriended by, in this order, a woman with two toy poodles that she hated (and spoke often and at high volumes about how much she despised them); a woman who dressed her schnauzer in a rotating-according-to-the-day-of-the-week array of colored tutus; and a woman who had a Westie, and though he was a male she had a hot-pink collar and harness for him and called him Katherine.

And then there was Barbara, a very pretty and extremely fit blond woman, outfitted in the nicest, newest items from Patagonia who strolled every morning with her spirited terrier mix. Barbara worked in PR and often sent me invitations to parties she was hosting for her client, a furrier. She'd get visibly annoyed when I politely declined. When, several polite declines later, she confronted me on why I never came to her parties, I said it was because I was against fur. She exhaled heavily and said that life was short and I needed to make more of it and never spoke to me again. I always wish I'd had the presence of mind to reply, "Life *is* short. Especially for the foxes."

And then, a few years into having a dog and walking her daily in Central Park, I did meet a guy. His name—if you've ever read a romance novel or glanced at the cover of one, then, here, hold on to your hat—was Fabio.

After several years of working completely from home, I needed financially and mentally to head back to work part time. I prepared to return three days a week to a beloved former boss. I was enthusiastic about every part of our arrangement: time in an office, out in the world, working for someone I enjoyed and admired, plenty of time left over in the week to write. However, one thing that I was not at all enthusiastic about, downright dismayed about in fact, was Carlie. Three days a week, my dog, who had grown accustomed to my constant company, would be—gasp!—alone.

If bringing Carlie to work with me had been an option, I would have brought her in a second. It was not even an inkling of an option. I hated the thought of leaving her alone in the apartment, all day, even if it was only three days a week. I determined that I would do everything I could to make the transition as easy as possible. I vowed to get up at six every morning so that we'd still have plenty of time to do our cherished morning walk. Still, I had to figure out the best thing to do with Carlie while I was at work. My mind, it boggled at the thought that the majority of dog owners in

New York had long been facing down this reality on a daily basis.

I'd taken Carlie to the doggie day care on my block for Yappy Hour several times. Though it is an all-around very nice facility, Carlie never seemed to like it much. I gathered this intel, sleuthlike, from the way she would stop short as we approached and attempt to run in the opposite direction. Also from the fact that once we were inside, Carlie was not so much enjoying Yappy Hour as she was sitting next to me, panting and shaking. I could not leave her there all day. I would get her a dog walker, and not just any dog walker, but a great one.

I knew nothing about dog walkers.

I'd taken Carlie on almost every walk she'd ever been on, and when I traveled she headed out to Long Island to be with my parents. In the few times I'd been away from home for an untenably long period of time during the day, one of my neighbors had chipped in. Though as lovely as the great majority of my neighbors are, even I, as I spiraled downward into a bit of dog-love-induced crazy, knew that asking a neighbor to walk Carlie on a daily basis would be a bit, well, shall we say, much. Also, and maybe this was the clincher, my neighbors had jobs.

The logical thing would be to ask my neighbors for the numbers of their dog walkers. But having worked from home, I'd seen these dog walkers in action. Like an overly vigilant mom on playground patrol, I'd witnessed my neighbor dogs tied to parking meters, yanked, walked by smokers and incessant cell phone talkers; I'd seen them *scolded*. A total Type B pet discipliner and someone who would sooner run into traffic than tie my dog up outside, I couldn't really see it working out with me and any of these dog walkers, let alone Carlie. I kept my eyes peeled in Central Park. I asked a few dog walkers for their cards, but none really struck me. I felt like I should wait, hold off, even though time was running out.

And then I saw him. I saw him, walking two long-haired dachshunds. He stood by happily, gently, kindly as the dachshunds sniffed. I've got more than a dash of the woo-woo in me, and I really very much believe in the energy people throw off. I believe that everyone could save themselves some trouble if only they would pay more attention to the energy that people throw off *like dogs do*. This dog walker's energy was peaceful. Nice. Calm. Gentle. Kind.

As the week progressed, and Carlie and I headed out into the neighborhood and to the park at varied times, I saw him standing by patiently as a border terrier smeared the entire side of his face in the grass. This man lovingly wiped him off with a soft cloth he removed from his pocket. I saw him bend down and pet the back of a golden retriever who was barking at a garbage can. I saw him lean in and whisper. He whispered assurances. I couldn't hear, but I was certain of it. The next day I approached him and I asked him his name. And his name was Fabio.

I asked him for his card. He gave it to me, his first and last difficult-to-pronounce name printed out, his cell phone number, his e-mail, a drawing of a dog in the upper right corner: a setter, I think. I pinned his card to the bulletin board over my desk the moment I got home. I called him shortly thereafter.

I asked him about his lunchtime availability and his rate. His availability was flexible. A half hour entailed a spin around the block. An hour meant a walk to Central Park and back. I wanted the hour, though his rate for such was high. Fabio suggested that Carlie could walk with other dogs for a lesser fee. Hmm, I thought Carlie might enjoy another dog or two. But maybe not more than that; I was unable to envisage her as one of those packs of dogs cruising en masse down city streets at the lunch hour. My dog is many things, all wonderful; "going with the flow" is not always one of them.

"How many other dogs?" I asked.

"Just one," he answered. "Sometime two."

We set up a date. First, Fabio would come over to my apartment, so my dog could meet him here, understand that he was welcome in her home. Then I'd give Fabio my keys and we'd be off to the races, or at least to a lunchtime walk to the park. The first meeting, suffice it to say, Carlie and Fabio hit it off. He crouched down low and said to her, in his very endearing Brazilian accent, "Hello, Carlie."

Carlie pasted her ears back and looked back up at him with ardor in her shiny black eyes and wagged her tail low.

She ran in a circle around my living room. I believed she did so to indicate joie de vivre. I handed over my keys.

"Okay, so Monday, Tuesday, Thursday?" Fabio confirmed.

"Yes." I nodded. "And you have my cell phone number?" I double-checked.

"I do." He nodded. He smiled kindly.

"And you'll call me if anything at all . . ." I trailed off, didn't want to dangerously jinx our new arrangement. "If you need anything," I amended.

"Yes." Fabio nodded. He took his cell phone out of his pocket and tilted it one way and then the other. "And you can always text me."

"You text?"

"Yes," he said. It sounded like "chess," and so it began. My text adventures with my dog walker.

I text him a lot. I text him to see how she's doing. I sit in my office and at lunchtime I reach for my phone and if it's raining, I text to see if she minded the rain.

Usually it is, "she walk fine." Once it was "Garlic walk well," and I realized that on her name, something had been lost in translation.

Once, sinking under the dual pressure of PMS and the fact that Carlie was scheduled for a teeth cleaning, I pretended she had been under the weather and I texted to see how she was feeling. Carlie wasn't under the weather at all. I just wanted to see a text about her.

"She is very happy," Fabio texted me. I trust that she is. Once or twice I've been home when he comes to take her. She barks at him, acts like a tough girl for my benefit. He looks down at her and says softly, sweetly, "Nooo."

Recently after I'd been away for a week and Carlie had been kicking it on Long Island, I texted Fabio to confirm that we'd be back on track that coming week. And who is to say he doesn't say this about all his girls, but this is what he texted me back: "We're on. I've missed her."

I texted back immediately: "I know she missed you, too."

Then. That November, after Carlie and Fabio had been together for a few months, my friend Courtney invited me to a dinner party she was hosting at her apartment. Courtney's apartment is lovely and only half a block away from an entrance to the park. I don't think I checked with Courtney as to the specifics of the party, but for whatever reason I had envisioned a very small, low-key affair: just me, Courtney, and the small handful of friends we had in common. At the end of the day, I didn't spruce up pre-party. I wore jeans and a boring gray sweater. I wore my glasses. I brought my gay best friend, Javi, with me.

When Javi and I walked into the party, I realized it was not a small affair at all, and I racked my mind for a reason as to why I had assumed it would be. Courtney's lovely park-adjacent apartment was brimming with people. As Javi and I approached a group and introduced ourselves, I shook the hand of a man I was sure I'd seen before but couldn't place.

His name didn't ring any bells. But I double-checked.

"Have we met before?" I asked.

"You know," he said, "I'm having trouble placing it. But I feel like I know you."

"Yes," I agreed. "Me, too."

We went through, quickly, where we went to college, worked, lived. There were no intersections, no crossovers, no communities that we could think of of which we'd both been a part. We left it for the moment. Later, as everyone moved to take their seats at the dining table, I heard him say something about his dog.

"Wait, you have a dog?" I asked over a few tableward-moving dinner party guests.

"Yes." He nodded. "Why? Do you?"

And then I knew how I knew him, and then I knew where I'd seen him before, and then I could remember seeing him almost every morning for the last five hundred, standing in a group of people in a clearing behind the Metropolitan Museum of Art throwing tennis balls for a gang of five, six Labradors. I'd seen this guy in Central Park every day, for years.

"Do you have a Lab?" I asked.

"Exactly," he said. "Clarence. How did you know?"

"I have a dog," I told him. "I walk her every morning in Central Park and I think, maybe, we've seen you there."

He narrowed his eyes. He tilted his head at me, the way a squirrel-hunting Jack Russell terrier might. "Do you have a Westie?"

"Exactly," I told him. He nodded his head.

As we arrived at the table, I noticed him change his trajectory, shifting his path so that he wound up standing right behind the chair that was next to the chair to which I had been, all along, headed. Javi, as gracious a friend as he is true, headed over to the other end of the table and, for the rest of the night, made his own way.

I took my seat. He took his. In the moments before Courtney clinked a piece of her silverware onto her crystal to make a predinner toast, he swiveled on his chair toward me.

"I knew I'd seen you before," he said, smiling.

That night, I didn't follow that dinner party rule where you're supposed to try to spend equal time talking to the dinner companions on either side of you. I only talked to him. It turned out he lived in Courtney's building, right down the hall. Clarence was his first dog, he hadn't grown up with dogs, and he loved everything about having a dog, except, as almost any New Yorker with a dog will tell you, the guilt.

After dinner, as everyone was complimenting Courtney and just starting to say good-bye and getting ready to go, he excused himself. I wondered. I might have worried. And then he returned about two minutes later with not one, but two Labradors.

Both dogs stood in the doorway to Courtney's apartment with their mouths slightly open, their eyes shiny and upward gazing and sweet in the way that almost all Labs' are. Their tails were swishing languidly and constantly behind them, their expressions at once expectant and slightly confused. I looked over at both of them, unsure as to which one was Clarence and who the other one was, since he hadn't mentioned a second dog—did he have two and just completely play favorites? I thought how I had, without ever really articulating it, always been a tremendous fan of the Lab.

Our eyes met. My eyes, his eyes, not mine and the Labs'. He explained to what remained of the assembled dinner party crowd that he was dog-sitting for one of Clarence's friends. Her name was Fetch. He smiled. I think I might have heard music cue up in the background.

As the last of Courtney's guests said good night and headed for the elevator, myself included, he came as well, to bring the dogs out for their last walk of the night. We got onto the elevator and he hooked a leash onto Fetch's collar but not onto Clarence's. I'd learn a few minutes later that Clarence was that rare, rare combination of New York City dog that was both super mellow and very obedient and went on walks around the block without needing a leash. As we left the building and emerged out on the sidewalk, brightly lit by lamps on either side of the building's entrance, I said good night.

"Do you have a card?" he asked me, and I thought for the

fiftieth, sixtieth, or at least seventeenth time that I really did need to get myself business cards. They had those MOO cards now, the charming mini ones where you could put your own design on the back. Behind him and to the left I saw Clarence sniffing right along the edge of the sidewalk. Next to him I saw Fetch, her tail swishing slowly back and forth, her gaze firm upon me, glazy and expectant, as if what she'd really like was for me not to have a business card, but rather a tennis ball, one that I would throw for her.

"Actually," I said, "I don't." I was tempted to add in that I really, truly didn't have business cards and that my saying I didn't have business cards was in no way an indication that I didn't want to hear from him because, actually, I did.

He reached into his back pocket. Fetch switched her gaze from me to him—*Maybe he has a ball!* I could almost hear her thinking. He pulled out his wallet and from it, a card, and handed it to me. I took it.

"Tell me your last name again?" he asked. I told him.

"I'll find you on Facebook."

Javi caught up, and we walked down Fifth Avenue and parted ways. Then I walked over to Madison Avenue to walk the few remaining blocks home. I took the card out of my pocket and glanced at it again. He worked in sports marketing. I put the card back in my pocket and thought how I'd never dated someone who worked in sports marketing. I'd dated a guy who sang in a band, a sommelier, a teacher, a photographer, an actor, a guy who got his dog to scratch on transfer paper and called it art and whose creative vision I greatly admired, but yet. I turned off Madison and onto my street and headed east toward my building.

He found me. On Facebook that is. He asked me, via e-mail, for my number. I thought that was nice, the fact that he wanted to take the time to talk on the phone, to have a real conversation. We talked on the phone, and we made plans to go to dinner. We picked a night the next week, the date was the first of the next month. He commented how he thought that was auspicious.

The next week when we met, on the first day of a new month, at a new Mexican restaurant in our neighborhood, a neighborhood which had, heretofore, really been wanting for good Mexican, the lighting in the restaurant was perfect. The noise level, too. There was sangria on the menu. With the exception of the slightly more than occasional very dirty martini, sangria has always been my favorite thing to drink. We sat down at a table toward the back of the room. As we did it made me think of a yoga teacher saying, "Let's all start at the back of our mats."

The man across the table from me had a very nice smile, and he loved his dog. I think it's always been the thing that makes it so that single people can keep going on dates when so many of them are awful: the possibility that the next one will be the one that clicks. The hope that a lot of the best stuff is still ahead. The belief that out there, somewhere, is someone who looks at the world and the things in it in a

similar way to you. Out there, somewhere, is someone who
might smile at you in a certain way so that you know, almost
immediately, that you have absolutely zero options but to
smile right back.

The waitress came by for drink orders. We both ordered
sangria. The conversation turned to dogs. Specifically to dog
walking.

"Do you work from home?" he asked.

"Two days a week," I told him. "Three days I'm in an
office."

"Who walks your dog when you're at the office?" he
asked me.

"I have a dog walker," I told him.

"Who do you use?"

"His name is Fabio," I said.

He looked right at me for a moment and then he looked
away, kind of wistfully off at the middle distance, for not
more than a millisecond; it was the kind of wayward off-
into-the-distance glance that had you not been paying attention, you would have missed. He turned back to me.

"Fabio," he said, and smiled. "The best dog walker in
Central Park."

I smiled back.

## ACKNOWLEDGMENTS

. . . . . . . . . . . . . . . . . . . . . . . . . . .

The ESSAYS! The book you hold in your hands (or, um, glimpse on your e-reader) is the end result of a four-year journey from farm to table that would not have been possible without the help of numerous friends, loved ones, colleagues, canines, neighbors, and people whose names have been changed.

For listening to me go on about the essays, say I was no longer writing the essays, announce that I was once again writing the essays, and spout earnest, misty-eyed clichés about the essays along the lines of, "you know, the only way through them is through them," I am very grateful to: Joe Veltre, Joanna Schwartz, Christine Ciampa, Cynthia Zabel, Greg Zabel, Javi Fuentes, Sarah Mlynowski, Robin Epstein, Lynn Parramore, Lauren Willig, Alfred Levitt, Liz Topp, Stacey Ballis, Trish Ryan, Elinor Lipman, Sherry Breslau, Jennifer Geller, Allison McCabe, Susan Roth, Phil Costanzo, Joey Pace, Jane Pace, and Michael Pace.

For their patience, care, and professionalism with this book and all that have preceded it, I'm so appreciative of the wonderful team at Berkley, most especially Susan Allison, Leslie Gelbman, Erin Galloway, Rita Frangie, Danielle Stockley, and Amy

# Acknowledgments

Schneider; also, Kara Burney, Alice Lawson, and everyone terrific at the Gersh Agency.

And thanks most of all to you, my readers, for making it so that my job is to hang out with my dog all day (and write things).

Printed in the United States
by Baker & Taylor Publisher Services